TRIUMPH or

A TRACT FO!

Books by David H.J.Gay referred to in this volume:

'A Gospel Church': A Warning.

Amyraut & Owen Tested: And Found Wanting.

Attracting Unbelievers to Church: Points to Ponder.

Battle for the Church: 1517-1644.

Christ Is All: No Sanctification by the Law.

Church: Performance or Participation?: Learning from the Lockdown.

Eternal Justification: Gospel Preaching to Sinners Marred by Hyper-Calvinism.

Evangelicals Warned: Isaiah 30 Speaks Today.

False Brothers: Paul and Today.

Infant Baptism Tested.

Luther on Baptism: Sacramentalism in the Raw.

New-Covenant Articles Volume Six.

New-Covenant Articles Volume Thirteen.

Public Worship: God-Ordained or Man-Invented?

Romans 11: A Suggested Exegesis.

Septimus Sears: A Victorian Injustice and Its Aftermath.

The Glorious New-Covenant Ministry: Its Basis and Practice.

*The Gospel Offer **Is** Free.*

The Pastor: Does He Exist?

The Priesthood of All Believers: Slogan or Substance?

The Upper Room Discourse: An Epoch-Changing Event.

Three Verses Misunderstood: Galatians 3:23-25 Expounded.

To Confront or Not to Confront?: Addresses to Unbelievers.

Relationship Evangelism Exposed: A Blight on the Churches and the Ungodly.

Undervalued Themes: Resurrection and Kingdom.

Triumph or Tragedy?

A Tract for the Times

...men who had understanding of the times, to know what Israel ought to do...

1 Chronicles 12:32

...wise men who knew the times...

Esther 1:13

David H.J.Gay

BRACHUS

BRACHUS 2024

Scripture quotations come from a variety of versions

There is no one who has left house or brothers or sisters or mother or father or children or lands, for my sake and for the gospel, who will not receive... now in this time... persecutions, and in the age to come eternal life

Mark 10:29-30

In the world you will have tribulation

John 16:33

...through many tribulations we must enter the kingdom of God

Acts 14:22

...that no one be moved by these afflictions. For you yourselves know that we are destined for this. For when we were with you, we kept telling you beforehand that we were to suffer affliction

1 Thess. 3:3-4

The grace of God has appeared... training us to renounce ungodliness and worldly passions, and to live self-controlled, upright, and godly lives in the present age, waiting for our blessed hope, the appearing of the glory of our great God and Saviour Jesus Christ

Tit. 2:11-13

All who desire to live a godly life in Christ Jesus will be persecuted, while evil people and impostors will go on from bad to worse, deceiving and being deceived

2 Tim. 3:12-13

I, John, your brother and partner in the tribulation and the kingdom and the patient endurance that are in Jesus...

Rev. 1:9

Contents

Note to the Reader 15
Introduction 19

TRAGEDY

The Last Days: When? 31
The Last Days: What? 35
The Early Days 37
Learning from Israel: The Principle 47
Learning from Israel: The History 55
The Future: What Did Christ Predict? 69
The Past 2000 Years 79

OBJECTIONS

Objections 89

TRIUMPH

Triumph 105

RESPONSIBILITIES

Responsibilities 133

APPENDICES

Appendix 1: Daniel 2:44 177
Appendix 2: Jonathan Edwards 183
Appendix 3: Crawford Gribben 191
Appendix 4: John Wesley 193
Appendix 5: B.W.Newton and H.Borlase 199
Appendix 6: The English Reformation 203

Note to the Reader

I wanted to write a book on 'The Fall of the Church'; or, more precisely, its consequences. By 'The Fall of the Church' I mean the way in which the original purity of the *ekklēsia* was ruined in the fourth century by Constantine in league with the Fathers, when between them they invented Christendom. That's what I wanted to write about. But, as I say, not simply to set out the historical fact. I wanted to write about the way this 'Fall' effects us today.[1]

But as I started to write, I soon became convinced that, despite the measure of truth which there is within the phrase, 'The Fall of the Church', this 'Fall' is, in fact, a myth. And it is a myth which had been staring me in the face all the time: the *ekklēsia* did not retain its purity until the fourth century, and then, as it were, in one calamitous step, plunge over the cliff, falling into ruin. Virtually from the word 'go', right from the time of the apostles, the *ekklēsia* was marred by man; and it has never recovered. That has become my conviction. This marring by man I see written large in Scripture; and played out in the subsequent history of the Church.

This does not mean that I no longer think that the Fathers and Constantine did immense harm to the *ekklēsia* and the gospel by setting up Christendom – 'The Fall of the Church' if you will – but I now see Christendom as but one of many downward steps – the worst of the lot, indeed – into the present ruinous state of the *ekklēsia*. Later centuries – including the twentieth and our own – have continued the plunging spiral.

---

[1] Without any design on my part, I can see that this present book is a kind of climax to several of my earlier works, works such as *Battle*; *Infant*; *The Pastor*; *The Priesthood*; *The Upper Room*, and various articles on topics relevant to what follows. And on a broader front, my works on the law, the new covenant and its implications come into this category.

Note to the Reader

From time to time, steps have been taken to try to rectify the position, but the decline continues.

Many disagree with me. They believe that the history of the church is a triumphant epic, even down to our own day.

Others – an increasing number, it seems to me – who, thinking that the present state of the church leaves a great deal to be desired, nevertheless claim that Scripture warrants us to expect a restitution or restoration of something like a 'Golden' time for the *ekklēsia*. Indeed, they have called upon a prophetical system – postmillennialism – to argue – with what at times seems like unbounded confidence – for a triumphant, glorious time for the *ekklēsia* before Christ returns. And, as far as I understand it, this coming 'Golden Age', in their opinion, will knock the apostolic time into a cocked hat! They anticipate an overwhelming revival, with a great number of Jews being converted, leading to a massive awakening among the Gentiles. Under this scheme, the three thousand of Pentecost (Acts 2:41), soon swelling by another two thousand (Acts 4:4), will be seen as a mere pinprick! The coming 'revival' will be world-wide!

While I am convinced that believers should always be striving to reform themselves (individually) and the *ekklēsia* (corporately), with the aim of recovering Christ's new-covenant pattern revealed in the post-Pentecost Scriptures (however far beyond reach that excellent aim might be in this fallen world), I vehemently discount any expectation of a triumphant spiritual kingdom *before* Christ returns.

Does this mean there is no hope? Far from it! Triumph – the triumphant fulfilment of God's eternal purpose – is certain.

All this I see in Scripture.

And that's the background to my book.

One other point. This book – the one that you are now are in danger of reading – was not written by an academic having a scholarly debate with other academics. No! It was written by an everyday sort of believer who was trying to set out what he sees

Note to the Reader

in Scripture, doing so in a way that might help other everyday believers come to terms with a difficult, but unavoidable, topic.

Introduction

With the outpouring of the Holy Spirit at Pentecost, the Lord Jesus Christ, as an integral part of the new covenant, brought into actual existence the *ekklēsia* which he had promised a while before (Matt. 16:18). At first, under the apostles, the believers enjoyed what might be called a 'Golden Age' (Acts 2:42-47; 4:32-37). But this time was short-lived. Before long, trouble broke out. The Jewish authorities vented their spleen against the infant *ekklēsia* (Acts 4:1-31). Then hypocrisy reared its loathsome head among the believers (Acts 5:1-11). That matter having been dealt with, in no time at all serious internal racial-disagreement erupted within the *ekklēsia* (Acts 6:1-6). That was put right. But then outright Jewish persecution was not long in coming, wreaking havoc among the believers, scattering them far and wide (Acts 6:8, and on). Of course, wherever these believers settled, assemblies sprang up. Nevertheless, it did not take long before Judaisers – false brothers, the *pseudadelphoi* – began to infiltrate the various assemblies, and their nefarious activities cost Paul, in particular, much anxiety. He not only personally experienced their disastrous intrusion among the believers in Antioch (Acts 14:24 – 15:35; Gal. 2:1-10), but he soon found that they were doing immense harm in almost every assembly.[1]

As for the trouble at Antioch, all had been well until the *pseudadelphoi* had appeared. But when they got to work, even Peter was affected. So much so, he stopped eating with Gentile believers, and Barnabas was swept along in his wake. Consequently, Paul had the heart-rending task of making a

---

[1] See my *False*. See my 'A Disaster Averted: Romans 14:5-6' on my sermonaudio.com page. Apostolic resistance to false teaching and false teachers is written large across the New Testament (Acts 15:1-35; Rom. 16:17-18; 2 Cor. 2:17; 4:2; 11:1-15; 1 Tim. 1:3-7; 6:3-10; 2 Tim. 3:1-5; 2 Pet. 2:1-22; 3:3-4; 1 John 2:18-27; 4:1-6; 2 John 7-11; Jude 3-23, for instance).

Introduction

public stand; which, for the sake of the gospel (Gal. 1:6-10; 2:4-5), he did:

> When Cephas [that is, Peter] came to Antioch, I opposed him to his face, because he stood condemned. For before certain men came from James, he was eating with the Gentiles; but when they came he drew back and separated himself, fearing the circumcision party. And the rest of the Jews acted hypocritically along with him, so that even Barnabas was led astray by their hypocrisy. But when I saw that their conduct was not in step with the truth of the gospel, I said to Cephas before them all: 'If you, though a Jew, live like a Gentile and not like a Jew, how can you force the Gentiles to live like Jews?' (Gal. 2:11-14).

Please note that the Spirit did not try to hide any of this. It was an episode in the sad endless saga of believers failing. And it is pleasing to read that with the passage of time a reconciliation took place.[2]

But, alas, this was not the only time Paul and Barnabas disagreed. The two men, with the blessing of the Antioch believers, took the problem of the *pseudadelphoi* back to where it belonged; namely, the *ekklēsia* in Jerusalem (after all, the trouble had only blown up in Antioch when 'certain men [had come] from James') (Acts 15:1-5). When all was settled (or so it seemed):

> ...Paul said to Barnabas: 'Let us return and visit the brothers in every city where we proclaimed the word of the Lord, and see how they are'. Now Barnabas wanted to take with them John called Mark. But Paul thought best not to take with them one who had withdrawn from them in Pamphylia and had not gone with them to the work. And there arose a sharp disagreement, so that they separated from each other. Barnabas took Mark with him and sailed away to Cyprus, but Paul chose Silas and departed, having been commended by the brothers to the grace of the Lord. And he went through Syria and Cilicia, strengthening the churches (Acts 15:36-41).

---

[2] See Col. 4:10; Philem. 24; 2 Tim. 4:11; 1 Pet. 5:13.

Introduction

And so it went on. Paul in the last chapter of his final letter to Timothy, showed that things had changed between him and Mark (had Mark benefitted by Paul's rebuke?). But that is not all it showed. Paul was lonely. He pleaded with Timothy, and the anxiety racking his heart is patent:

> Do your best to come to me soon. For Demas, in love with this present world, has deserted me and gone to Thessalonica. Crescens has gone to Galatia, Titus to Dalmatia. Luke alone is with me. Get Mark and bring him with you, for he is very useful to me for ministry. Tychicus I have sent to Ephesus. When you come, bring the cloak that I left with Carpus at Troas, also the books, and above all the parchments. Alexander the coppersmith did me great harm; the Lord will repay him according to his deeds. Beware of him yourself, for he strongly opposed our message. At my first defence no one came to stand by me, but all deserted me. May it not be charged against them! But the Lord stood by me and strengthened me, so that through me the message [that is, the preaching of God's revelation, God's word] might be fully proclaimed and all the Gentiles might hear it. So I was rescued from the lion's mouth. The Lord will rescue me from every evil deed and bring me safely into his heavenly kingdom. To him be the glory forever and ever. Amen (2 Tim. 4:9-18).

No! It was not all sunshine in the apostolic day.

As for conversions under gospel preaching, the contrast between Acts 2 – 4:4; 6:7; 9:35,42; 12:24 with Acts 17 and Acts 28:17-31 is palpable. In the early days, the preachers of the gospel saw many converts under their preaching. Within a few years, it was not so. I am not saying there was no blessing (Acts 19:10,20), but conversion-work, in general, became much tougher, and less successful.

But it was in-house where the real trouble lay, within the *ekklēsia*.[3] Although Paul definitively demolished the teaching and principles of the *pseudadelphoi* – and we have his arguments laid out in Scripture – as the years passed, again and

---

[3] See my 'The Church Attacked: When, and Without or Within?' in my *New-Covenant Articles Volume Thirteen*.

Introduction

again their descendants would re-appear in assembly after assembly.

And, let us not forget, Christ had severe criticisms and warnings for most of the seven *ekklēsia* of Asia Minor (Rev. 2 & 3).

I have not finished with the way the *ekklēsia* degenerated during the time of the apostles, but since this is but the 'Introduction' I leave it there – for the moment.

False teachers seem to possess the mythological power of the Lernaean Hydra![4] In particular, during the second to the fifth centuries the theological philosopher-politicians known as the Fathers ruled the churches, and they grievously and irreparably adulterated the new covenant by going back to the old covenant and making that the norm and pattern for the *ekklēsia* and the gospel. They also adopted pagan ideas.[5] In other words, they Judaised and paganised the new covenant. If all that were not enough, bitter Roman persecution was unleashed against the believers throughout the Empire.

This catalogue of trouble came to a head in the fourth century with the 'end' of Roman persecution brought about by the so-called conversion of the Emperor, Constantine. But the price tag was excessive: the *ekklēsia* suffered a massive, root-and-branch alteration. Constantine, and a later Emperor, Theodosius I, in cahoots with Church dignitaries, made Christianity the State religion, forging Church and State into one religious-political commonwealth, a Judaised-cum-Paganised juggernaut. The *ekklēsia* has never recovered from this devastating move.

What do today's believers think of the history of the *ekklēsia* these past 2000 years? If believers think about those years at all, I guess most of them think that while the church – however 'the church' might be defined – has had some very serious times of crisis, rocky decades – even centuries – in the main the

---

[4] According to the Greek legend, when one head of the monster was cut off, two grew in its place.
[5] See my *The Pastor; Battle*.

Introduction

needle has always swung back to the right upward course. Their key supporting texts (though, in my view, they are commonly misunderstood) are probably found in the prophecy of Daniel and in the words of Christ:

> In the days of those kings the God of heaven will set up a kingdom that shall never be destroyed, nor shall the kingdom be left to another people. It shall break in pieces all these kingdoms and bring them to an end, and it shall stand forever (Dan. 2:44).[6]

And:

> I will build my church, and the gates of hell shall not prevail against it (Matt. 16:18).[7]

Some believers, however, go further; much further. They think the last 2000 years have been – admittedly with some downs – a history of growing prosperity and expansion for the church and the spread and influence of the gospel.[8] They gladly sing – should that be '*glibly* sing'? – the words of Sabine Baring-Gould:

> *Like a mighty army*
> *Moves the church of God;*
> *Brothers, we are treading*
> *Where the saints have trod.*
> *We are not divided,*
> *All one body we,*
> *One in hope and doctrine,*
> *One in charity.*

---

[6] See Appendix 1.

[7] A much debated statement. I think 'the gates of hell (Hades)' refers to death (Job. 38:7; Isa. 38:10); the *ekklēsia* – nor, of course, individual believers – will ever be defeated by death. I will come back to this.

[8] Jonathan Edwards, for one: 'By each of these comings of Christ [that is, events in church history], God works a glorious deliverance for his church. Each of them is accompanied with a glorious advancement of the state of the church' (Jonathan Edwards: *History of Redemption*). See Appendix 2.

Introduction

Really? How then, one wonders, can they also sing these words by Samuel John Stone:

> *Though with a scornful wonder,*
> *Men see her sore oppressed,*
> *By schisms rent asunder,*
> *By heresies distressed...*

Others think the last 2000 years – especially since the introduction of Christendom – have been, in general, a time of fearful defection from the gospel.[9]

Roman Catholics see the past 2000 years as a time of much progress for the Roman Church as – so they believe – Christ has continued to reveal new truth by the Spirit; that is, he has, they think, revealed that new truth to the ruling party – the Curia – of the Roman Church.[10]

And what about the future for the *ekklēsia*? How do most believers see that? What do they think Scripture tells us to expect? Some think that Scripture promises a glorious history

---

[9] John H.Gerstner: 'My conviction as a student of Scripture and of church history is that most of the latter is a departure from the former' (John H.Gerstner: 'Handout Church History, Conclusion notes 8 and 9'). For other witnesses, see Appendices 3, 4 and 5.

[10] In 1845, John Henry Newman published *An Essay on the Development of Christian Doctrine*. Newman used the idea of [the] development of doctrine to defend Roman Catholic teaching from attacks by those who saw certain elements in Catholic teaching as corruptions or innovations. He relied on an extensive study of the early Fathers to trace the elaboration or development of doctrine which he argued was in some way implicitly present in divine revelation; that is, as he saw it, in Scripture and Tradition. Newman's thinking had a major impact on the Second Vatican Council and appears in its statement that 'the understanding of the things and words handed down grows through the contemplation and study of believers... which tends continually towards the fullness of divine truth' (adapted from Wikipedia). Stephen K.Ray: 'Development of doctrine is a key and crucial responsibility of the Church' (Stephen K.Ray: *Crossing the Tiber: Evangelical Protestants Discover the Historical Church*, Ignatius Press, San Francisco, 1997, Mumbai 2010 edition, p71).

Introduction

for the church preceding Christ's return – a time, if not of unbroken and rising prosperity, at least a period when the church will flourish, so that, when Christ returns he will find a church, a kingdom, that is a mighty power in the world, exercising untold influence for good. To be specific, such believers envisage the widespread conversion of Jews leading to a widespread conversion of Gentiles, signalling the triumph of the kingdom. One way such believers justify this is by funnelling a host of Old Testament prophecies into Romans 11, seemingly ignoring – or not even noticing – Paul's stated purpose in writing Romans 9 – 11, or the way the post-Pentecost writers use those prophecies.[11]

Others think almost the very opposite – that Scripture speaks of the preservation of a faithful minority – the remnant[12] – while the professing church in general will be guilty of appalling widespread apostasy. While they can envisage occasional bright spots, they anticipate a general defection from the apostolic gospel. Things will get even worse before Christ comes.

Yet others seem to take refuge in their expectation of a 1000 year Jewish kingdom centred on Jerusalem with Christ as king. The preceding time has simply to be endured.

---

[11] See Iain H.Murray: *The Puritan Hope: Revival and the Interpretation of Prophecy*, The Banner of Truth Trust, Edinburgh, 1971. For my response, see my *Romans 11*. I have taken the following from the blurb for a Texas Conference to be held in 2024: 'America will have Christ, or it will have chaos. All over the world, Christians are waking up to this reality. Many are embracing the idea of "Christian Nationalism"'. 'At this conference, we'll be focusing on the blueprint for establishing the New Christendom. Seven doctrines for ruling the world'. Hmm.

[12] The remnant in the day of the new covenant is not the so-called invisible church within the visible, like the faithful in the nation of Israel in the day of the old covenant (see 'Lloyd-Jones Interview with Aneirin Talfan Davies'), but believers in the world, especially in Christendom.

Introduction

These are the kind of questions and issues I am concerned with in this book.

But let me make it clear that I want to write nothing more than a brief introductory tract for believers who have hardly – if ever – really explored Scripture on such things.[13] They have, maybe, simply absorbed the received wisdom and tradition in which they find themselves. That, and 'the church' they 'attend', is the norm, and it has been ever thus, and ever will be, world without end. If nothing else, I hope my work may disabuse them of this and provoke them to take off the blinkers and adopt a Berean spirit, and eagerly search the Scriptures to see if these things are so (Acts 17:11).

* * *

Let me summarise where we are. For those who have thought about these matters, opinions are sharply divided into two main camps: those who see the church's history (past, present and future) as glorious – tempered, of course, by seasons of setbacks – but in the main, one of triumphant progress. This group divides again: some fall back on the comfortable cop-out of the Reformed invention of visible and invisible churches;[14]

---

[13] I am not being modest when I say that many others are better qualified to tackle these themes, but I feel compelled to throw my two mites into the treasury.

[14] See my *Infant*. Emil Brunner, writing in 1952, commenting on the difference between the *ekklēsia* of the New Testament and the church of today, said: 'It is... a well-known fact that dogmatists and church leaders [not excepting evangelicals – DG]... are only too ready to bridge the gulf between "then" [that is, the New Testament] and "now" [that is, our present experience] by a handy formula such as that of development [that is, Newman's "solution"], or by appealing to the distinction between the [so-called – DG] visible and invisible church, and thus to give a false solution to this grave and distressing problem. But while many theologians and church elders are able to quieten their consciences by such formulae, others are so much the more aware of the disparity between the Christian fellowship of the apostolic age and our own "churches", and cannot escape the impression that there may perhaps be something wrong with what we

Introduction

the visible carries all the downside, and the invisible all the good. Evangelicals including the Reformed, while they may not be eager to admit it, expect development, as God reveals more truth to succeeding generations in the church,[15] and this allows them to add evangelical glosses – visible and invisible church, house of God, ecclesiastical structures, synods, and the like – all for so-called advance, of course.[16] On the other hand, there are those who look upon the history of the church as a record of how man has molested the work of God, thereby causing untold damage. This, of course, does not mean that nothing good has come this past 2000 years, but the general course of the church has been depressing, at the very least. As for the future, such believers are much struck by Christ's rhetorical question:

> When the Son of Man comes, will he find faith on earth? (Luke 18:42).

In this work I want to try to encourage thought on such issues.

---

now call the church' (Emil Brunner: *The Misunderstanding of the Church*, Lutterworth Press, London, 1952, pp5-6). With the passage of seventy years, things have not come any closer to a resolution. Calvin, following Cyprian, taught that outside the church there is no salvation. Brunner rightly dismissed this: 'The idea of the invisible church is foreign to the New Testament, while the interpretation of the real visible church as a merely external means of salvation is not only foreign to it but completely impossible... The thought of Calvin, that the church is an external support for faith, is utterly unintelligible... The *ekklēsia* of the New Testament... is precisely not that which every "church" is at least in part – an institution, a something. The Body of Christ is nothing other than a fellowship of persons... where fellowship... signifies a common participation a togetherness, a community life. The faithful are bound to each other through their common sharing in Christ and in the Holy Ghost, but that which they have in common is precisely no "thing", no "it", but a "he", Christ and his Holy Spirit... The Body of Christ... has nothing to do with an organisation and has nothing of the character of the institutional about it' (Brunner pp9-11; see also Brunner pp14-18).

[15] Such believers are adopting Newman's idea – see earlier notes.

[16] The list is endless: the moral law, threefold division of the law, Christian sabbath... For Stephen K.Ray's list, taunting evangelicals, see Ray pp42-43.

Introduction

Why should we be interested? Well, what we think about such things seriously affects our present way of living, and the way we face the future – no mean consequences.

TRAGEDY

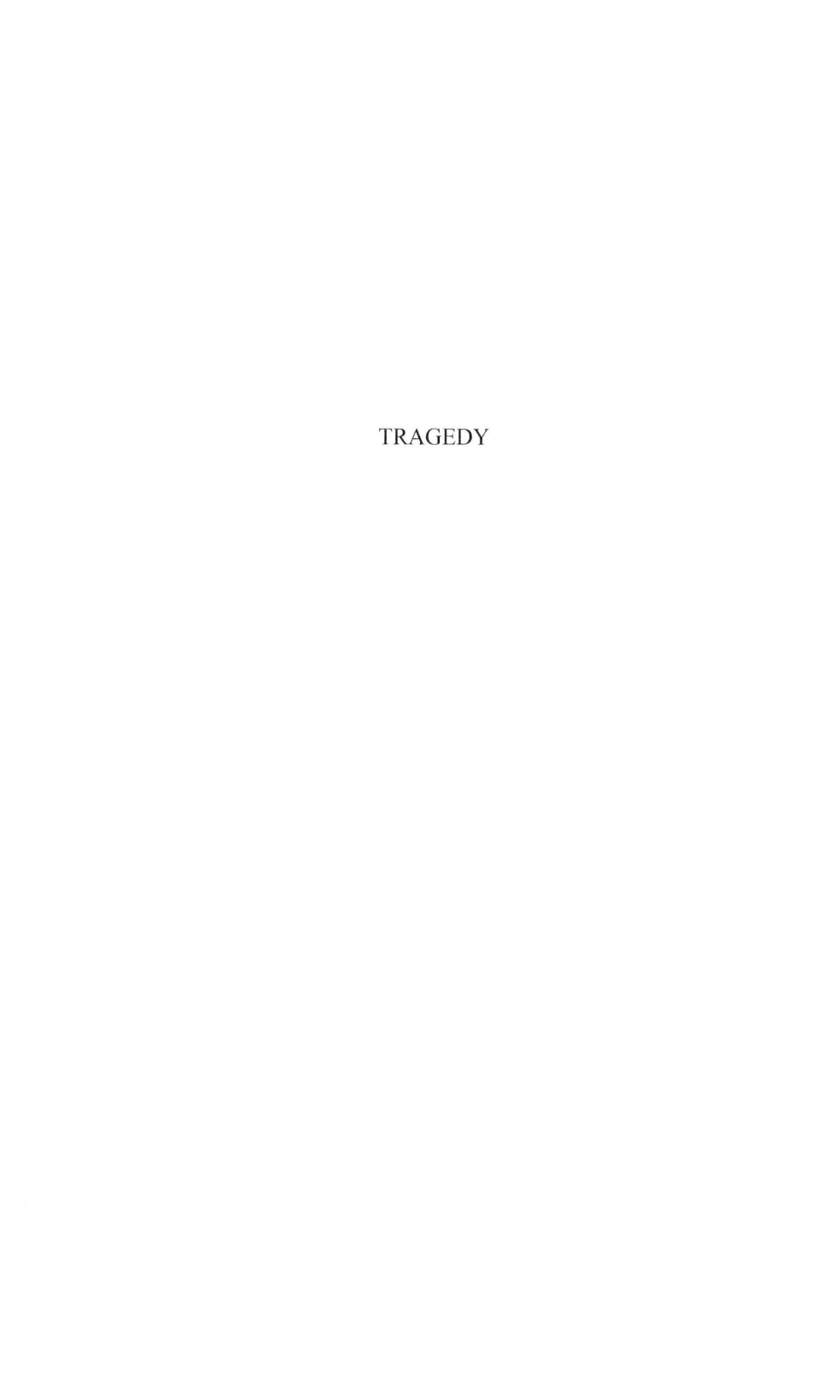

The Last Days: When?

I start with the key scriptural phrase – 'the last days'. What does Scripture mean by it? Believers not infrequently use the phrase – what do they understand by it? Are the two the same? Often – nearly always, in my experience – they are not. When, bemoaning the dire spiritual straits in which we find ourselves today, many believers will solemnly wag their head and mutter: 'Well, it's the last days, you know!' What they mean is that they think that Christ is about to come again, and that Scripture tells them that the final days before his appearing will be appalling – this is what we are to expect, and that's where we are. Is that what Scripture means by 'the last days'?

No!

On the day of Pentecost, Peter, quoting Joel, applied the prophet's words to what was happening at that very moment in Jerusalem. He clearly saw the events of the day of Pentecost as signalling 'the last days':

> ...this [that is, that which was happening as he spoke, that very day] is what was uttered through the prophet Joel: 'And in ***the last days*** it shall be, God declares, that I will pour out my Spirit on all flesh...' (Acts 2:16-17).

For Peter, 'the last days' had begun with the outpouring of the Spirit on the day of Pentecost.

He was not alone in that view.

The writer to the Hebrews regarded the public ministry of Christ as signalling the start of 'the last days'. I do not concede that when he spoke 'these last days' he simply meant 'recently'. We know that the writer's purpose was to set out the contrast between the old age and the new, the old covenant and the new, with the superiority of the new over the old. For the writer, the appearance of Christ in the world marked the watershed between the two 'times'. The writer of Hebrews was setting the tone for his entire treatise – the superiority of the new covenant over the old – when he wrote:

> Long ago, at many times and in many ways, God spoke to our fathers by the prophets, but in *these last days* he has spoken to us by his Son... (Heb. 1:1-2).

And he could not have put it any stronger when he wrote:

> [Christ] has appeared once for all at *the end of the ages* to put away sin by the sacrifice of himself (Heb. 9:26).

And the same goes for Peter's letter:

> [Christ]... was made manifest in *the last times* for the sake of you... (1 Pet. 1:20).

John was clear:

> It is *the last hour*, and as you have heard that antichrist is coming, so now many antichrists have come. Therefore we know that it is *the last hour*. They [apostates, that is] went out from us, but they were not of us; for if they had been of us, they would have continued with us. But they went out, that it might become plain that they all are not of us (1 John 2:18-19).

I break in to draw attention to the link John made between 'the last hour' and the appearance of antichrists. John – and his readers – knew it was 'the last hour' because of the appearance of antichrists.[1] I will return to this.

To continue: Paul could tell the Corinthians that the details of Israel's failures and sins during the days of the old covenant:

> ...were written down for our instruction [that is, for the instruction of the apostle and his fellow-believers], on whom *the end of the ages* has come (1 Cor. 10:11).

---

[1] Many believers limit 'antichrist' to a man who will appear at the end of the age – 'The Antichrist'. Such a man – 'the man of lawlessness' – will come (2 Thess. 2:1-12). But as Paul stated in that passage: 'The mystery of lawlessness is already at work' (2 Thess. 2:7).

The Last Days: When?

The point is surely established: there are two ages, two times – before the first appearance of Christ and after his first appearance; the two times being – speaking broadly – the time of the old covenant and the time of the new. When Christ appears a second time, of course, 'the last time' will be swallowed up in the eternal age. The material point, however, is this: whatever Scripture tells us about the state of the gospel in the world, and the condition of the *ekklēsia*, during (that is, throughout) 'the last time', 'the last days', it is telling us about things today. Moreover, when Scripture speaks of 'the last days' it tells us what things were like yesterday – right back to Pentecost – what they are like today, and what they will be like tomorrow – until Christ comes. 'The last days' are this present age, 'this present time' (Rom. 8:18), the age of the new covenant, the time in which we are living. In short, now. It is quite wrong to limit 'the last days' to the few months just before Christ returns.

This is no small point. It will play a major role in what follows.

The Last Days: What?

We have seen what the New Testament means by 'the last days'; that is, the 'when'. And 'the last days' stretch from Pentecost to the return of Christ. But, of course, the next question to be answered concerns the character of this age, what we are to expect during this time. In other words, what does Scripture tell us about the state of the gospel and the *ekklēsia* in the world in 'these last times'; that is, what does Scripture tell us about the spiritual ambience we are to expect throughout this age, from Pentecost until Christ's return in glory?

It is explicit:

> Now the Spirit expressly says that in ***later times*** some will depart from the faith by devoting themselves to deceitful spirits and teachings of demons, through the insincerity of liars whose consciences are seared (1 Tim. 4:1-2).

> But understand this, that in ***the last days*** there will come times of difficulty. For people will be lovers of self, lovers of money, proud, arrogant, abusive, disobedient to their parents, ungrateful, unholy, heartless, unappeasable, slanderous, without self-control, brutal, not loving good, treacherous, reckless, swollen with conceit, lovers of pleasure rather than lovers of God, having the appearance of godliness, but denying its power. Avoid such people (2 Tim. 3:1-5).[1]

> You should remember the predictions of the holy prophets and the commandment of the Lord and Saviour through your apostles, knowing this first of all, that scoffers will come in ***the last days*** (2 Pet. 3:3-4).

> You must remember, beloved, the predictions of the apostles of our Lord Jesus Christ. They said to you: 'In ***the last time*** there will be scoffers, following their own ungodly passions'.

---

[1] Clearly, these dreadful things were happening in the early days: it is hard to see how Timothy could 'avoid' men and women who would be not be living until at least 2000 years after he had died!

The Last Days: What?

It is these who cause divisions, worldly people, devoid of the Spirit (Jude 17-19).

Bearing in mind what we have already seen, these extracts do not mean that during the last few months before the return of Christ, things will go pear-shaped. No! They tell us that throughout this age, the *ekklēsia* will pass through choppy waters. And worse.

Notice that these indictments are not to be confined to pagans; professing believers are involved.

* * *

This leaves us with the obvious question, the unavoidable decision. In light of the above, what is your verdict? Would you say that the apostles told us that the course of the gospel during this age – until Christ returns – would be one of Triumph or Tragedy? Of course, it's not either/or, black or white. Nevertheless which of the two better fits the bill?

The Early Days

As we have seen, the first believers were living in 'the last days' – as we are; further, we have seen that 'the last days' are marked by apostasy. So what was life like in the early *ekklēsia*? In this chapter, I will set out how the New Testament records the way in which this alarming picture of 'the last days' was played out in those early days, showing how the scriptural warnings about 'the last days' applied as much in the very early days as they do now – and, consequently what we are to expect in our time. The early *ekklēsia* lived surrounded by a sea of various cultures – all hostile – and it was under constant attack, both from without and from within.[1] Let me prove it.

As I have already noted, Acts records the sad and rapid way in which the *ekklēsia* was marred, even in the time of the apostles.[2] And the attacks were not confined to the believers in Jerusalem. I said I would return to this.

One can almost put it like this: which of the apostolic letters are not concerned with – dealing with, correcting – some kind of sinful disorder in behaviour, doctrine, whatever, in the *ekklēsia*? Paul was explicit about Scripture; he was far from seeing Scripture as a mere treasury of promises, designed to soothe believers in their difficulties. While I do not deny 'the encouragement (comfort) of the Scriptures' (Rom. 15:4), as Paul stated, Scripture also has a much sterner role to play:

> All Scripture is breathed out by God and profitable for teaching, for reproof, for correction, and for training in righteousness, that the man of God may be complete, equipped for every good work (2 Tim. 3:16-17).

---

[1] See my 'The Church Attacked: When, and Without or Within?' in my *New-Covenant Articles Volume Thirteen*.
[2] For sake of completeness, I will have to return to one or two passages already quoted.

The Early Days

Note that: 'for reproof, for correction, and for training in righteousness, that the man of God may be complete, equipped for every good work' not 'for making the believer feel good about himself, excusing every carnal desire he may have, that the man of God may be happy at all times', confident that, no matter how carnal he is now, a glorious eternity awaits him.

Several letters were concerned with warnings and rebukes, or the machinations of false teachers who were infiltrating the *ekklēsia*. Take Galatians, 2 Corinthians, Hebrews, 2 Peter and Jude, as examples. Indeed, it would be quicker to tackle the matter the other way about, and list the books which had no such warnings and corrections!

Other letters, however, were more concerned with troubles arising from within. Paul, when bidding farewell to the Ephesian elders, was blunt about what was causing him alarm. Yes, there would be infiltration from outside; but that was not all:

> I know that after my departure fierce wolves will come in among you, not sparing the flock; and from among your own selves will arise men speaking twisted things, to draw away the disciples after them. Therefore be alert, remembering that for three years I did not cease night or day to admonish every one with tears (Acts 20:29-31).[3]

Yes, internal trouble would mar many assemblies.[4]

As a clear case of disorder, take the *ekklēsia* at Corinth. Paul rebuked the believers at Corinth for disunity, quarrelling over personalities (1 Cor. 1:11), carnality (1 Cor. 3:1-4), boasting (1 Cor. 4:6-8), poor or non-existent spiritual discipline (1 Cor. 5), a willingness to pursue their own interests in law against fellow-believers, and that before pagans (1 Cor. 6:1-8), sexual sin (1 Cor. 6:15-20), idolatry (1 Cor. 8), disorder in their

---

[3] Paul's fears were, alas, justified. Mark the difference between his letter to the Ephesians and Rev. 2:1-7.
[4] See my 'The Church Attacked: When, and Without or Within?' in my *New-Covenant Articles Volume Thirteen*.

The Early Days

assemblies, including carnality at the Lord's supper (1 Cor. 10-11,14), misuse of spiritual gifts (1 Cor. 12-14), lack of love (1 Cor. 13) and error over the resurrection (1 Cor. 15).

And that's just the apostle's first letter to that one *ekklēsia*! Elsewhere, I have explored Paul's way of countering false brothers in Antioch, Galatia and Corinth[5] – yes, in addition to the grim list in the previous paragraph, the *ekklēsia* at Corinth was infested with false brothers, and the Corinthians were buying into their teaching! The *ekklēsia* at Corinth was far from faultless!

Take the *ekklēsia* in Galatia. The apostle was staggered at the rapidity of the defection in Galatia:

> I am astonished that you are so quickly deserting him who called you in the grace of Christ and are turning to a different gospel (Gal. 1:6).

And he was explicit:

> Because of false brothers secretly brought in – who slipped in [had infiltrated our ranks, had sneaked in among us] to spy out our freedom that we have in Christ Jesus, so that they might bring us into slavery – to them we did not yield in submission even for a moment, so that the truth of the gospel might be preserved for you (Gal. 2:4-5).

Indeed, it was false teaching and the rapid spread of false gospels throughout the various *ekklēsia* – not just in Corinth and Galatia – that constituted one of Paul's greatest headaches, if not heartaches. One sick man in a room of healthy people does not catch 'wellness' from the healthy, but one sick man can infect an entire room of people. So it is with error: one bad apple in the barrel will ruin the lot, one blighted tuber will rapidly spread the infestation to the entire sack of potatoes. Just so with false teachers and their false gospels. Paul was constantly on the *qui vive*, stamping on the fires of error wherever they erupted, forever alert to the danger. Already – in Paul's day – false Christs and false gospels abounded, spread

---

[5] See my *False*.

The Early Days

by the preaching and writing of the false teachers. And believers were being seduced by such teachers and their false Christs and false gospels.

As the apostle told the Corinthians:

> If someone comes and proclaims another Jesus than the one we proclaimed, or if you receive a different spirit from the one you received, or if you accept a different gospel from the one you accepted, you put up with it readily enough (2 Cor. 11:4).

As we have seen, he felt it necessary to tell the Galatians of his anguish:

> I am astonished [he wrote] that you are so quickly deserting him who called you[6] in the grace of Christ and are turning to a different gospel – not that there is another one, but there are some who trouble you and want to distort the gospel of Christ. But even if we or an angel from heaven should preach to you a gospel contrary to the one we preached to you, let him be accursed. As we have said before, so now I say again: If anyone is preaching to you a gospel contrary to the one you received, let him be accursed. For am I now seeking the approval of man, or of God? Or am I trying to please man? If I were still trying to please man, I would not be a servant of Christ. For I would have you know, brothers, that the gospel that was preached by me is not man's gospel (Gal. 1:6-11).

As he told Timothy:

> Remain at Ephesus so that you may charge certain persons not to teach any different doctrine, nor to devote themselves to myths and endless genealogies, which promote speculations rather than the stewardship from God that is by faith. The aim of our charge is love that issues from a pure heart and a good conscience and a sincere faith. Certain persons, by swerving from these, have wandered away into vain discussion, desiring to be teachers of the law, without understanding either what

---

[6] There has been much debate over 'him who called you'; I take this to be God the Father, by the Spirit, effectually calling sinners to Christ (John 3:3-8; 6:37,40,44; Rom. 8:26-30; 1 Cor. 1:9; Gal. 1:15-16; 5:5,6,8; 1 Thess. 2:12; 5:23-24).

The Early Days

they are saying or the things about which they make confident assertions (1 Tim. 1:3-7).

Paul warned the Thessalonians:

> Now concerning the coming of our Lord Jesus Christ and our being gathered together to him, we ask you, brothers, not to be quickly shaken in mind or alarmed, either by a spirit or a spoken word, or a letter seeming to be from us, to the effect that the day of the Lord has come. Let no one deceive you in any way. For that day will not come, unless the rebellion comes first, and the man of lawlessness is revealed, the son of destruction, who opposes and exalts himself against every so-called god or object of worship, so that he takes his seat in the temple of God, proclaiming himself to be God. Do you not remember that when I was still with you I told you these things? And you know what is restraining him now so that he may be revealed in his time. For the mystery of lawlessness is already at work. Only he who now restrains it will do so until he is out of the way. And then the lawless one will be revealed, whom the Lord Jesus will kill with the breath of his mouth and bring to nothing by the appearance of his coming. The coming of the lawless one is by the activity of Satan with all power and false signs and wonders, and with all wicked deception for those who are perishing, because they refused to love the truth and so be saved. Therefore God sends them a strong delusion, so that they may believe what is false, in order that all may be condemned who did not believe the truth but had pleasure in unrighteousness (2 Thess. 2:1-12).

Do not miss the reference to 'the lawless one' – The Antichrist. I have already drawn attention to the term in John's first letter when he was dealing with the antichrists in his day (1 John 2:18-19; see also 1 John 4:3). And Paul said that The Antichrist will arise just before the second coming of Christ. Antichrists and their teaching were alive and active in the time of the first believers, are alive and active today, and will still be virulent and active right up until the appearance of Christ.

No wonder Paul warned Timothy:

> Keep a close watch on yourself and on the teaching. Persist in this, for by so doing you will save both yourself and your hearers (1 Tim. 4:16).

And:

> Avoid irreverent babble, for it will lead people into more and more ungodliness, and their talk will spread like gangrene. Among them are Hymenaeus and Philetus, who have swerved from the truth, saying that the resurrection has already happened. They are upsetting the faith of some (2 Tim. 2:16-18).

And:

> I charge you in the presence of God and of Christ Jesus, who is to judge the living and the dead, and by his appearing and his kingdom: preach the word; be ready in season and out of season; reprove, rebuke, and exhort, with complete patience and teaching. For the time is coming when people will not endure sound teaching, but having itching ears they will accumulate for themselves teachers to suit their own passions, and will turn away from listening to the truth and wander off into myths. As for you, always be sober-minded, endure suffering, do the work of an evangelist, fulfil your ministry (2 Tim. 4:1-5).

As he explained, he had suffered from the defection of professed believers; and how it pained him! He pleaded with Timothy:

> Do your best to come to me soon. For Demas, in love with this present world, has deserted me and gone to Thessalonica... Luke alone is with me... At my first defence no one came to stand by me, but all deserted me (2 Tim. 4:9-16).

Paul gave Titus his marching orders:

> This is why I left you in Crete, so that you might put what remained into order... For an overseer, as God's steward... must hold firm to the trustworthy word as taught, so that he may be able to give instruction in sound doctrine and also to rebuke those who contradict it.
> For there are many who are insubordinate, empty talkers and deceivers, especially those of the circumcision party. They must be silenced, since they are upsetting whole families by teaching for shameful gain what they ought not to teach... Therefore rebuke them sharply, that they may be sound in the faith, not devoting themselves to Jewish myths and the

commands of people who turn away from the truth. To the pure, all things are pure, but to the defiled and unbelieving, nothing is pure; but both their minds and their consciences are defiled. They profess to know God, but they deny him by their works. They are detestable, disobedient, unfit for any good work (Tit. 1:5-16).

And Peter left his readers in no doubt about what they should expect:

> False prophets also arose among the people, just as there will be false teachers among you, who will secretly bring in destructive heresies, even denying the Master who bought them, bringing upon themselves swift destruction. And many will follow their sensuality, and because of them the way of truth will be blasphemed. And in their greed they will exploit you with false words (2 Pet. 2:1-3).

John warned his readers:

> Beloved, do not believe every spirit, but test the spirits to see whether they are from God, for many false prophets have gone out into the world (1 John 4:1).

Jude was awake to it:

> Beloved, although I was very eager to write to you about our common salvation, I found it necessary to write appealing to you to contend for the faith that was once for all delivered to the saints. For certain people have crept in [secretly slipped in, wormed their way in] unnoticed who long ago were designated for this condemnation, ungodly people, who pervert the grace of our God into sensuality and deny our only Master and Lord, Jesus Christ (Jude 3-4).

And as Christ rebuked the *ekklēsia* at Pergamum:

> You have some there who hold the teaching of Balaam, who taught Balak to put a stumbling block before the sons of Israel, so that they might eat food sacrificed to idols and practice sexual immorality. So also you have some who hold the teaching of the Nicolaitans. Therefore repent. If not, I will come to you soon and war against them with the sword of my mouth (Rev. 2:14-16).

The Early Days

And what about the Laodicean *ekklēsia*? What a boon for preachers – excellent source material for an emotional gospel address to sinners, with the ready-made literal illustration to hand, care of William Holman Hunt.[7] When all the time, the main thrust of Christ's words are directed to the local assembly of believers in Laodicea, and, by extension, churches today. Seen in that light, Christ's words are not so comfortable, are they? They read:

> I know your works: you are neither cold nor hot. Would that you were either cold or hot! So, because you are lukewarm, and neither hot nor cold, I will spit you out of my mouth. For you say, I am rich, I have prospered, and I need nothing, not realising that you are wretched, pitiable, poor, blind, and naked. I counsel you to buy from me gold refined by fire, so that you may be rich, and white garments so that you may clothe yourself and the shame of your nakedness may not be seen, and salve to anoint your eyes, so that you may see. Those whom I love, I reprove and discipline, so be zealous and repent. Behold, I stand at the door and knock. If anyone hears my voice and opens the door, I will come in to him and eat with him, and he with me. The one who conquers, I will grant him to sit with me on my throne, as I also conquered and sat down with my Father on his throne. He who has an ear, let him hear what the Spirit says to the churches (Rev. 3:15-22).

And, don't forget, there are five other churches in those two chapters! While not all of Christ's words were critical, think how completely – and rapidly – the seven churches which Christ addressed all vanished. In particular, I say it again, how dramatic must have been the nose-dive at Ephesus (from Acts 20 and Ephesians to Revelation 2).

And as for Jewish and Gentile persecution of believers in the early days, let me give one example. Take the *ekklēsia* at Thessalonica:

> You, brothers, became imitators of the churches of God in Christ Jesus that are in Judea. For you suffered the same things from your own countrymen as they did from the Jews, who

---

[7] The sentimental representation of Christ as the light of the world.

The Early Days

> killed both the Lord Jesus and the prophets, and drove us out, and displease God and oppose all mankind by hindering us from speaking to the Gentiles that they might be saved – so as always to fill up the measure of their sins...
> Therefore when we could bear it no longer, we were willing to be left behind at Athens alone, and we sent Timothy, our brother and God's co-worker in the gospel of Christ, to establish and exhort you in your faith, that no one be moved by these afflictions. For you yourselves know that we are destined for this. For when we were with you, we kept telling you beforehand that we were to suffer affliction, just as it has come to pass, and just as you know. For this reason, when I could bear it no longer, I sent to learn about your faith, for fear that somehow the tempter had tempted you and our labour would be in vain (1 Thess. 2:14 – 3:5).

> We ought always to give thanks to God for you, brothers, as is right, because your faith is growing abundantly, and the love of every one of you for one another is increasing. Therefore we ourselves boast about you in the churches of God for your steadfastness and faith in all your persecutions and in the afflictions that you are enduring.
> This is evidence of the righteous judgment of God, that you may be considered worthy of the kingdom of God, for which you are also suffering – since indeed God considers it just to repay with affliction those who afflict you, and to grant relief to you who are afflicted as well as to us, when the Lord Jesus is revealed from heaven with his mighty angels in flaming fire, inflicting vengeance on those who do not know God and on those who do not obey the gospel of our Lord Jesus (2 Thess. 1:3-8).

In addition to the point I am making here – that the days of the early *ekklēsia* were no bed of roses – notice the comfort Paul offered the believers at Thessalonica: the return of Christ. Nothing about a glorious time for the *ekklēsia* before Christ's return. Nothing about 'heaven when you die'. But all about the return of Christ.

Is all this not evidence enough to show that those who think that the early *ekklēsia* existed in some sort of insulating aura of perfection need to seriously re-think?

The Early Days

* * *

This leaves us with the question, the decision. In light of the above, reader, what is your verdict? Would you say the course of the gospel during the early years of this age was one of Triumph or Tragedy? Of course, it wasn't either/or, black or white. Nevertheless which of the two would best fit the bill? Can Tragedy be ruled out altogether?

Learning from Israel: The Principle

The story thus far: we have seen the way in which the *ekklēsia* was severely mauled almost from the start; we have also seen that that the post-Pentecost writers of Scripture predicted that this age will be marked by severe trouble for believers, that defection from the gospel will be a sure sign of this age.

Do we have any further evidence to help us in our thinking about all these points, to confirm us in thinking that we believers will be exposed to spiritual danger? Even more, to confirm us in the view that apostasy from the new covenant by believers is certain? (My use of tautological *litotes* is deliberate, for emphasis – only believers can be guilty of apostasy). Do we have any further evidence?

We certainly do. Those same writers made it very clear that believers have a great deal of scriptural information to guide them in their thinking: the history of Israel under the old covenant.

Before we get into the detail, let us stand back and face the big picture. This is always the wisest thing to do: indeed, it is essential to take on board the general, before homing in on the specific. What am I talking about?

The Old Testament is, if I may put it like this, the 'bigger half' of the Bible. The old covenant has been fulfilled by Christ and rendered obsolete – obsolete as an active covenant, that is. Israel, as a nation, has served its God-ordained purpose.[1] So why do believers – who patently are not the nation of Israel, who are not under the old covenant, who are not under the Mosaic law – why do believers have a Bible which has, as its larger part, a record of the nation of Israel under that old, obsolete covenant and its law?

---

[1] For my arguments, see, for instance, my *Christ*; *The Upper Room*.

Learning from Israel: The Principle

The New Testament faces this question head on. Please let that register. It faces it because it has to! Let that sink in. Under the Reformed system, the Bible is a flat book, all parts of which are equally relevant to Israel and 'the church'. Indeed, because Israel and the *ekklēsia* are 'one church'; Israel was 'the Old Testament church', and the *ekklēsia* is 'the New Testament church', essentially one and the same church. The old and new covenants are really one covenant in two administrations. This is how the Reformed read the Bible. And this is why the Reformed need never ask why believers have an Old Testament. For those who sing nothing but the psalms, who sprinkle their babies on the basis of circumcision, who demand that believers keep the Jewish sign (Ex. 16; 20:8-11; 31:12-17; Neh. 9:13-15; Ezek. 20:12,20) of the sabbath (albeit adjusted in accordance with Reformed covenant-theology), and so on, the question never crosses their mind. But, as I say, the writers of the post-Pentecost Scriptures knew they had to deal with this vital question. And so they did!

That is the big picture.

Let me say a little more.

Paul was adamant. Despite the undoubted fact that the nation of Israel was not 'the church', that Israel was not under the new covenant, even so:

> ...whatever was written in former days [that is, especially the history of Israel in the days of the old covenant] was written for our instruction (Rom. 15:4).

'Our instruction or learning'? Who were the 'our'? Paul meant believers in his day – and ever after, until the end of time – during 'the last days'. The first believers – whether they were Jews or Greeks – had to learn from Israel's history; and so do we, living as we do, as the first believers were, in the days of the new covenant. We have not grown out of it. Nor will we – until Christ returns. Israel's history – under a different covenant – serves as a standing warning, example – 'instruction' – to believers under their covenant. Not that believers are under the Mosaic law. No, that is never said anywhere in Scripture.

Learning from Israel: The Principle

Indeed, Scripture asserts expressly that believers are not under the law (Rom. 6:14-15; 7:4-6; 1 Cor. 9:20; Gal. 2:19; Eph. 2:15; Col. 2:14). Nevertheless, whatever can be found in the Old Testament is, in some way or another, an illustration for believers in the days of their covenant, the new covenant. Thus said Paul.

The general principle, I remind you, is this:

> All Scripture [all – both Old and New Testaments] is breathed out by God and profitable for teaching, for reproof, for correction, and for training in righteousness, that the man of God may be complete, equipped for every good work (2 Tim. 3:16-17).

Clearly believers – in the apostle's day and now – have to learn from Israel's history. How did Israel respond under their covenant, the old, Mosaic covenant? What can we learn from their mistakes, their history?

That's the general, overall picture, the big picture. But the post-Pentecost writers brought their teaching into much sharper focus than that!

As we have already seen, Paul could tell the Corinthians that the details of Israel's failures and sins in the time of the old covenant:

> ...were written down for our instruction, on whom the end of the ages has come [that is, living as we do in the days of the new covenant] (1 Cor. 10:11).

How important a statement is that! Israel's history could not be more relevant today. Alas, as Georg Hegel said: 'The only thing that we learn from history is that we learn nothing from history'. Let that not be true of us! Consequently, we need to look at Israel's history, see what it tells us, and what we must learn from it, even though the old covenant under Moses has been fulfilled by Christ, and thus been superseded by the new covenant. And by 'it', I mean far more than the particular episodes selected by Paul in 1 Corinthians 10; the whole of

Israel's history under its covenant – the Mosaic – is instructive for believers in this regard.[2]

Since it has such a major role to play in the matter in hand, let me quote the full context of Paul's statement to the Corinthians:

> For I do not want you to be unaware, brothers, that our fathers were all under the cloud, and all passed through the sea, and all were baptised into Moses in the cloud and in the sea, and all ate the same spiritual food, and all drank the same spiritual drink. For they drank from the spiritual Rock that followed them, and the Rock was Christ. Nevertheless, with most of them God was not pleased, for they were overthrown in the wilderness.
> Now these things took place as examples for us, that we might not desire evil as they did. Do not be idolaters as some of them were; as it is written: 'The people sat down to eat and drink and rose up to play'. We must not indulge in sexual immorality as some of them did, and twenty-three thousand fell in a single day. We must not put Christ to the test, as some of them did and were destroyed by serpents, nor grumble, as some of them did and were destroyed by the Destroyer. Now these things happened to them as an example, but they were written down for our instruction, on whom the end of the ages has come. Therefore let anyone who thinks that he stands take heed lest he fall. No temptation has overtaken you that is not common to man. God is faithful, and he will not let you be tempted beyond your ability, but with the temptation he will also provide the way of escape, that you may be able to endure it (1 Cor. 10:1-13).

Israel was not the church, of course. As I have already implied, this will sound strange – even, mad, crazy – to Reformed readers of my book (if there are any), those who mistakenly see the old and new covenants as virtually one covenant in two administrations. But it is the truth! Israel was not the old-

---

[2] In Paul's warning commands to the *ekklēsia* – 'Do not grieve the Holy Spirit of God, by whom you were sealed for the day of redemption' (Eph. 4:30) and 'Do not quench the Spirit' (1 Thess. 5:19) – can we not hear the prophet's complaint of Israel who 'rebelled and grieved [God's] Holy Spirit' (Isa. 63:10)?

Learning from Israel: The Principle

covenant church; it was Israel.[3] There was no such thing as the old-covenant church; that is the figment of Reformed theologians. Israel was Israel. God formed the nation of Israel to be his old-covenant people; that is, he chose the pagan Abram, made him a believer, justified him by faith, re-named him Abraham, and from his descendants – Isaac, Jacob, and so on – brought forth the nation of Israel centuries after Jacob's descendants, who had gone down into Egypt in time of famine, had descended into slavery, and had to endure the slaughter of their male offspring by their Egyptian tyrants (Ex. 1:8-22). It was God who, through Moses, led his people out of Egyptian bondage into freedom in the time of the exodus, thereby forming them into a nation – the nation of Israel. God distinguished this nation from all others (Deut. 4:6-45; 5:26; 7:6-11; Ps. 147:19-20; Acts 2:23; Rom. 3:2; 9:4; 1 Cor. 9:20-21) by giving them his covenant at Sinai – the old covenant – and its law, which covenant was to last until the coming of the Messiah (Gal. 3:23-26).[4]

The children of Israel knew God's promise – conditional on their obedience:

> If you will indeed obey my voice and keep my covenant, you shall be my treasured possession among all peoples, for all the earth is mine; and you shall be to me a kingdom of priests and a holy nation (Ex. 19:5-6)...

...and they were prepared to give God their solemn vow of obedience to all that God made known to them:

> ...all that the LORD has spoken we will do (Ex. 19:8)...

---

[3] See my *Christ*; *Infant*; *'A Gospel Church'*; *Battle*. Many serious mistakes follow the mingling of the two covenants: circumcision misguidedly sets the pattern for baptism, so baby-sprinkling replaces the dipping of believers; as Israel was a mixed community, so for those who mingle the covenants, the church is a designedly-mixed conglomeration of the regenerate and unregenerate. And so on.

[4] See my *The Upper Room*; *Three*.

...and, furthermore, they were given the clearest of instruction under Moses (Ex. 20 – 40), and repeated warnings and pleadings from the prophets.

Yet, even so, the children of Israel proved themselves serial breakers of the old covenant.[5] As God would later explain through Hosea:

> They have transgressed my covenant and rebelled against my law (Hos. 8:1).

In short, after leaving Egypt, Israel spent forty years in the literal wilderness while an entire adult generation (apart from two) perished: 'With most of them God was not pleased, for they were overthrown in the wilderness' (1 Cor. 10:5). But the stark truth is, apart from occasional bright spots, the history of Israel from the exodus until AD70 can be described as a pitiful journey through a howling spiritual wilderness.

So much so, God, having divided Israel into two – the northern and the southern kingdoms – took both into captivity. The northern kingdom, because of its incessant transgression of the covenant under an unbroken line of evil kings, was hauled into captivity under Assyria, and never heard of again as a nation. The southern kingdom, Judah, though it had a few kings who did show marks of obedience, eventually went into captivity under Babylon, but after an exile lasting 70 years, was restored to the land. The restoration, however, fell far short of the glory of the kingdom under Solomon. After Malachi, Judah had no prophet for four centuries, not a word from God, until John the Baptist. In AD70, Jerusalem was sacked by the Romans, the temple was destroyed, and the nation of Judah, as the old-covenant people of God, ceased to exist. The entire system fell with Christ's fulfilment of the old covenant which rendered it obsolete (Heb. 8:13).

And that, in a nutshell, is the sad history that the apostle told us must serve as a warning to believers; the Jews' grim response

---

[5] See my *Evangelicals*.

under the old covenant must serve as a warning to believers about their response to God under the new covenant.

In light of all that I have argued in this chapter, there remains only one course open to believers today. We have to get to grips with the Old Testament. We have to understand Israel's history. We have to see the lessons, the illustrations, the warnings, the examples which are set out in the books of Moses, the prophets, and all the rest. And we have to learn those lessons. More, we have to apply those lessons to our own lives and circumstances – all in the light of the new covenant, of course.

And that takes us to the next chapter.

Learning from Israel: The History

The exodus under Moses signalled the beginning of Israel as a nation. Moreover, within a few weeks of their leaving Egypt, God gave the Israelites his covenant at Sinai. A privileged people, indeed! A distinguished, separated people! As we have seen, the Israelites, assembled in anticipation under the mountain, were as keen as mustard, freely promising full obedience to God's revelation of the covenant to them through Moses :

> Moses came and called the elders of the people and set before them all these words that the LORD had commanded him. All the people answered together and said: 'All that the LORD has spoken we will do' (Ex. 19:7-8).

But, as the 17th-century English proverb has it, fine words butter no parsnips.[1] Words are cheap; actions cost more; and count more! And in any case – even in the short time since Moses had returned to the Israelites in Egypt, ending his time in Midian, armed with God's promise of deliverance – the people had shown how quickly they could switch from euphoria to doubt, depression and grumbling (as detailed in Exodus 4 – 17).[2] Their track record was far from promising.

And so it proved at Sinai: even before the ink (as it were) had dried on the contract, even *before* they had received the law of the covenant, the Israelites in effect broke it by making a calf-idol under Aaron's direction. This was immediately followed by Moses smashing the two tablets, leading to the slaughter of many Israelites (Ex. 32). What a disastrous start to the age of the old covenant!

---

[1] Making fine promises is easy; what counts is the doing of what is promised. As the old saw has it, actions speak louder than words.
[2] As those chapters show, Moses himself was not exempt.

Learning from Israel: The History

For a brief – but penetratingly honest – outline of what was to come, I turn to Stephen. When put on trial by the Jews, in his defence – rather, his attack – he resolutely hammered home unpalatable truth; the Jews were treating Stephen as their forefathers had treated Moses (and, of course, Christ). Stephen responded:

> This Moses, whom they rejected, saying: 'Who made you a ruler and a judge?' – this man God sent as both ruler and redeemer by the hand of the angel who appeared to him in the bush. This man led [the Israelites] out, performing wonders and signs in Egypt and at the Red Sea and in the wilderness for forty years. This is the Moses who said to the Israelites: 'God will raise up for you a prophet like me from your brothers'. This is the one who was in the congregation in the wilderness with the angel who spoke to him at Mount Sinai, and with our fathers. He received living oracles to give to us. Our fathers refused to obey him, but thrust him aside, and in their hearts they turned to Egypt, saying to Aaron: 'Make for us gods who will go before us. As for this Moses who led us out from the land of Egypt, we do not know what has become of him'. And they made a calf in those days, and offered a sacrifice to the idol and were rejoicing in the works of their hands. But God turned away and gave them over to worship the host of heaven, as it is written in the book of the prophets: 'Did you bring to me slain beasts and sacrifices, during the forty years in the wilderness, O house of Israel? You took up the tent of Moloch and the star of your god Rephan, the images that you made to worship; and I will send you into exile beyond Babylon' (Acts 7:35-43).

Stephen, of course, was drawing on such passages as Numbers 11 – 14, in which Moses faithfully recorded Israel's failures – sins – that came in rapid succession after Sinai, including their unbelief at Kadesh Barnea. That particular sin – when they refused to believe God's promise, and act upon it – meant that almost an entire generation of Israelites was wasted as the nation wandered in the wilderness under God's judgment until the disobedient had perished (Ezek. 20:5-26,36). So much so, only two adult Israelites who had been at Sinai survived the wilderness (Num. 14:20-38). Furthermore, even after Israel had crossed the Jordan, Canaan was never fully conquered. Joshua recorded Israel's (and his) failures over Ai and Gibeon *etc.* Having seen what was going on all around him, and reading the writing on the wall, it is no wonder that Joshua adopted the tone he did in his last sermon. He well-knew that Israel still hankered after (as they chose fondly to remember them) the fleshpots of Egypt. He remembered that under Moses 'the rabble... had a strong craving' (Num. 11:4). And he remembered what the people had said, even with weeping as they expressed their feelings:

> Oh that we had meat to eat! We remember the fish we ate in Egypt that cost nothing, the cucumbers, the melons, the leeks, the onions, and the garlic. But now our strength is dried up, and there is nothing at all but this manna to look at (Num. 11:4-6).

The record speaks volumes. Joshua declared:

> Now therefore fear the LORD and serve him in sincerity and in faithfulness. Put away the gods that your fathers served beyond the River and in Egypt, and serve the LORD. And if it is evil in your eyes to serve the LORD, choose this day whom you will serve, whether the gods your fathers served in the region beyond the River, or the gods of the Amorites in whose land you dwell. But as for me and my house, we will serve the LORD.

The people glibly replied:

> Far be it from us that we should forsake the LORD to serve other gods, for it is the LORD our God who brought us and our fathers up from the land of Egypt, out of the house of slavery, and who did those great signs in our sight and preserved us in all the way that we went, and among all the peoples through whom we passed. And the LORD drove out before us all the peoples, the Amorites who lived in the land. Therefore we also will serve the LORD, for he is our God.

Joshua was not fooled! He did not take their promises at face value, and he pulled no punches in telling them so:

> You are not able to serve the LORD, for he is a holy God. He is a jealous God; he will not forgive your transgressions or your sins. If you forsake the LORD and serve foreign gods,

then he will turn and do you harm and consume you, after having done you good.

Nevertheless, the people remained defiant and self-confident:

> No, but we will serve the LORD.

Joshua spelled out what was involved in their vows:

> You are witnesses against yourselves that you have chosen the LORD, to serve him.

The people remained supremely confident:

> We are witnesses.

But Joshua had not finished:

> Then put away the foreign gods that are among you, and incline your heart to the LORD, the God of Israel.

Still the people were adamant:

> The LORD our God we will serve, and his voice we will obey.

Joshua did all he could to make their commitment watertight:

> So Joshua made a covenant with the people that day, and put in place statutes and rules for them at Shechem. And Joshua wrote these words in the book of the law of God. And he took a large stone and set it up there under the terebinth that was by the sanctuary of the LORD.

And he did not mince his words:

> Behold, this stone shall be a witness against us, for it has heard all the words of the LORD that he spoke to us. Therefore it shall be a witness against you, lest you deal falsely with your God.

And in this spirit, he brought the day to a close:

> So Joshua sent the people away, every man to his inheritance (Josh. 24:14-28).

So much for all that! But, as I say, despite their fine words, Joshua had not been fooled. He could see what was coming. Israel's rapid, sinful descent and betrayal of the covenant after

Learning from Israel: The History

Joshua's death is graphically recorded in the book of Judges; the history is abominable, some of it hardly fit for public reading.

And so it went on and on. Israel's history is a record of lowering clouds with occasional rays of watery, temporary sunshine, flattering to deceive. Prophet after prophet rebuked the people, calling them to repentance and reform. All to little avail. Or none! The kingdom divided, with both kingdoms eventually descending into captivity on account of their spiritual adultery.

The psalmist has supplied us with a graphic account of the apostasy of the old-covenant people. It is a long extract – and with good reason: Israel's sins were seemingly endless. Their rebellion began, as we have seen, even at the exodus from Egypt. This is how the psalmist put it as he admitted Israel's grim history before God:

> Our fathers, when they were in Egypt, did not consider your wondrous works; they did not remember the abundance of your steadfast love, but rebelled by the sea, at the Red Sea. Yet he saved them for his name's sake, that he might make known his mighty power. He rebuked the Red Sea, and it became dry, and he led them through the deep as through a desert. So he saved them from the hand of the foe and redeemed them from the power of the enemy. And the waters covered their adversaries; not one of them was left. Then they believed his words; they sang his praise.
> But they soon forgot his works; they did not wait for his counsel. But they had a wanton craving in the wilderness, and put God to the test in the desert; he gave them what they asked, but sent a wasting disease among them.
> When men in the camp were jealous of Moses and Aaron, the holy one of the LORD, the earth opened and swallowed up Dathan, and covered the company of Abiram. Fire also broke out in their company; the flame burned up the wicked.
> They made a calf in Horeb and worshipped a metal image. They exchanged the glory of God for the image of an ox that eats grass. They forgot God, their Saviour who had done great things in Egypt, wondrous works in the land of Ham, and awesome deeds by the Red Sea. Therefore he said he would

destroy them – had not Moses, his chosen one, stood in the breach before him, to turn away his wrath from destroying them.
Then they despised the pleasant land, having no faith in his promise. They murmured in their tents, and did not obey the voice of the LORD. Therefore he raised his hand and swore to them that he would make them fall in the wilderness, and would make their offspring fall among the nations, scattering them among the lands.
Then they yoked themselves to the Baal of Peor, and ate sacrifices offered to the dead; they provoked the LORD to anger with their deeds, and a plague broke out among them. Then Phinehas stood up and intervened, and the plague was stayed. And that was counted to him as righteousness from generation to generation forever.
They angered him at the waters of Meribah, and it went ill with Moses on their account, for they made his spirit bitter, and he spoke rashly with his lips.
They did not destroy the peoples, as the LORD commanded them, but they mixed with the nations and learned to do as they did. They served their idols, which became a snare to them. They sacrificed their sons and their daughters to the demons; they poured out innocent blood, the blood of their sons and daughters, whom they sacrificed to the idols of Canaan, and the land was polluted with blood. Thus they became unclean by their acts, and played the whore in their deeds.
Then the anger of the LORD was kindled against his people, and he abhorred his heritage; he gave them into the hand of the nations, so that those who hated them ruled over them. Their enemies oppressed them, and they were brought into subjection under their power. Many times he delivered them, but they were rebellious in their purposes and were brought low through their iniquity (Ps. 106:7-43).

God reminded Jeremiah of Israel's miserable track record, thus preparing him for the prophetic message he was to deliver to the people:

> I brought you [that is, Israel] into a plentiful land to enjoy its fruits and its good things. But when you came in, you defiled my land and made my heritage an abomination (Jer. 2:7).

As God could say, he had been clear in his command and promise, and had not over-burdened the nation:

> In the day that I brought them out of the land of Egypt, I did not speak to your fathers or command them concerning burnt offerings and sacrifices. This command I gave them: 'Obey my voice, and I will be your God, and you shall be my people. And walk in all the way that I command you, that it may be well with you'. But they did not obey or incline their ear, but walked in their own counsels and the stubbornness of their evil hearts, and went backward and not forward. From the day that your fathers came out of the land of Egypt to this day, I have persistently sent all my servants the prophets to them, day after day. Yet they did not listen to me or incline their ear, but stiffened their neck. They did worse than their fathers (Jer. 7:22-26).

Note that:

> ***From the day that your fathers came out of the land of Egypt to this day***, I have persistently sent all my servants the prophets to them, day after day.

But all in vain! Indeed, with the passing of time, things went from bad to worse. And God declared:

> The children of Israel and the children of Judah have done nothing but evil in my sight from their youth [that is, since they were made a nation at the exodus]. The children of Israel have done nothing but provoke me to anger by the work of their hands, declares the LORD. This city has aroused my anger and wrath, from the day it was built to this day, so that I will remove it from my sight because of all the evil of the children of Israel and the children of Judah that they did to provoke me to anger – their kings and their officials, their priests and their prophets, the men of Judah and the inhabitants of Jerusalem. They have turned to me their back and not their face. And though I have taught them persistently, they have not listened to receive instruction. They set up their abominations in the house that is called by my name, to defile it. They built the high places of Baal in the Valley of the Son of Hinnom, to offer up their sons and daughters to Molech, though I did not command them, nor did it enter into my mind,

that they should do this abomination, to cause Judah to sin (Jer. 32:30-35).

And, as a consequence, in Jeremiah's day, Judah would be hauled into captivity. And God warned the prophet what he should expect by way of indignant reaction when the people heard the news; more, he told Jeremiah what he had to say in response:

> And when you tell this people all these words, and they say to you: 'Why has the LORD pronounced all this great evil against us? What is our iniquity? What is the sin that we have committed against the LORD our God?' then you shall say to them: 'Because your fathers have forsaken me', declares the LORD, 'and have gone after other gods and have served and worshipped them, and have forsaken me and have not kept my law, and because you have done worse than your fathers, for behold, every one of you follows his stubborn, evil will, refusing to listen to me. Therefore I will hurl you out of this land into a land that neither you nor your fathers have known, and there you shall serve other gods day and night, for I will show you no favour' (Jer. 16:10-13).

As God had declared to the northern kingdom, Israel, through Hosea:

> Call his [that is, Hosea's second son's] name 'Not my People', for you [that is, Israel] are not my people, and I am not your God (Hos. 1:9).

And:

> When Israel was a child, I loved him, and out of Egypt I called my son. The more they were called, the more they went away; they kept sacrificing to the Baals and burning offerings to idols... They shall not return to the land of Egypt, but Assyria shall be their king, because they have refused to return to me (Hos. 11:1-5).[3]

Although the southern kingdom, Judah, was restored after seventy years in Babylon, things were never the same (Ezra 3:12-13).

---

[3] Among many other passages, see Ezek. 20:1-32.

And so it went on. The post-exile prophets had their work cut out trying to raise Judah to what she ought to have been. In vain! Things had plummeted to such a depth that God used Malachi to lay a very heavy charge against the restored people – the restored people, please note, even *after* their restoration from captivity:

> 'A son honours his father, and a servant his master. If then I am a father, where is my honour? And if I am a master, where is my fear?' says the LORD of hosts to you, O priests, who despise my name. But you say: 'How have we despised your name?' 'By offering polluted food upon my altar'. But you say: 'How have we polluted you?' 'By saying that the LORD's table may be despised. When you offer blind animals in sacrifice, is that not evil? And when you offer those that are lame or sick, is that not evil? Present that to your governor; will he accept you or show you favour?' says the LORD of hosts. 'And now entreat the favour of God, that he may be gracious to us. With such a gift from your hand, will he show favour to any of you?' says the LORD of hosts. 'Oh that there were one among you who would shut the doors, that you might not kindle fire on my altar in vain! I have no pleasure in you', says the LORD of hosts, 'and I will not accept an offering from your hand... You profane it when you say that the Lord's table is polluted, and its fruit, that is, its food may be despised. But you say: "What a weariness this is", and you snort at it', says the LORD of hosts. 'You bring what has been taken by violence or is lame or sick, and this you bring as your offering! Shall I accept that from your hand?' says the LORD (Mal. 1:6-13).

Do not miss the arrogance of the people: 'How... How... What a weariness... You snort...'.

As for the priests, God let them know what was in store for them unless things improved:

> I will send the curse upon you and I will curse your blessings. Indeed, I have already cursed them, because you do not lay it to heart. Behold, I will rebuke your offspring, and spread dung on your faces, the dung of your offerings, and you shall be taken away with it... The lips of a priest should guard knowledge, and people should seek instruction from his

Learning from Israel: The History

mouth, for he is the messenger of the LORD of hosts. But you have turned aside from the way. You have caused many to stumble by your instruction. You have corrupted the covenant of Levi, says the LORD of hosts, and so I make you despised and abased before all the people, inasmuch as you do not keep my ways but show partiality in your instruction (Mal. 2:2-9).

And so on...

But – how amazing it is – in the midst of this catastrophic declension, God had still preserved a remnant among them:

> Those who feared the LORD spoke with one another. The LORD paid attention and heard them, and a book of remembrance was written before him of those who feared the LORD and esteemed his name. 'They shall be mine', says the LORD of hosts, 'in the day when I make up my treasured possession, and I will spare them as a man spares his son who serves him. Then once more you shall see the distinction between the righteous and the wicked, between one who serves God and one who does not serve him' (Mal. 3:16-18).

But it was only a remnant:

> In that day the remnant of Israel and the survivors of the house of Jacob will no more lean on him who struck them, but will lean on the LORD, the Holy One of Israel, in truth. A remnant will return, the remnant of Jacob, to the mighty God. For though your people Israel be as the sand of the sea, only a remnant of them will return (Isa. 10:20-22).

> Isaiah cries out concerning Israel: 'Though the number of the sons of Israel be as the sand of the sea, only a remnant of them will be saved, for the Lord will carry out his sentence upon the earth fully and without delay'. And as Isaiah predicted: 'If the Lord of hosts had not left us offspring, we would have been like Sodom and become like Gomorrah'...
> Israel [as a whole] failed to obtain what it was seeking. The elect obtained it, but the rest were hardened... I do not want you to be unaware of this mystery, brothers: a partial hardening has come upon Israel (Rom. 9:27-29; 11:7,25).

After Malachi, the Jews had to endure 400 years of silence from God. And when Messiah appeared among them, in the main they rejected him (John 1:10-11), even crucifying him!

John, when referring to Christ's raising of Lazarus, recorded Jewish intrigue, even at the highest level, so that in their hatred they could scheme how to get the Romans to do the dirty work and kill Christ for them (Acts 2:23):

> Some of them [that is, the Jews] went to the Pharisees and told them what Jesus had done. So the chief priests and the Pharisees gathered the council and said: 'What are we to do? For this man performs many signs. If we let him go on like this, everyone will believe in him, and the Romans will come and take away both our place and our nation'. But one of them, Caiaphas, who was high priest that year, said to them: 'You know nothing at all. Nor do you understand that it is better for you that one man should die for the people, not that the whole nation should perish'. He did not say this of his own accord, but being high priest that year he prophesied that Jesus would die for the nation, and not for the nation only, but also to gather into one the children of God who are scattered abroad. So from that day on they made plans to put him [that is, Jesus] to death (John 11:46-53).

Christ let the Jews know that he was not ignorant of what was going on. By means of parable,[4] he confronted them with their hatred of him, and their plans to see it put into action:

> There was a master of a house who planted a vineyard and put a fence around it and dug a winepress in it and built a tower and leased it to tenants, and went into another country. When the season for fruit drew near, he sent his servants to the tenants to get his fruit. And the tenants took his servants and beat one, killed another, and stoned another. Again he sent other servants, more than the first. And they did the same to them. Finally he sent his son to them, saying: 'They will respect my son'. But when the tenants saw the son, they said to themselves: 'This is the heir. Come, let us kill him and have his inheritance'. And they took him and threw him out of the vineyard and killed him. When therefore the owner of the vineyard comes, what will he do to those tenants? (Matt. 21:33-40).

---

[4] No nice story for children!

Learning from Israel: The History

As he went on to tell them, Scripture – the word of God to Israel – had predicted it:

> Have you never read in the Scriptures: 'The stone that the builders rejected has become the cornerstone; this was the Lord's doing, and it is marvellous in our eyes'? (Matt. 21:42).

As Peter, in his turn told the Jews:

> This Jesus is the stone that was rejected by you, the builders, which has become the cornerstone (Acts 4:11).

As Israel had begun, so Israel went on. At the start of his letter, Jude summed it up:

> Now I want to remind you, although you once fully knew it, that the Lord,[5] who saved a people out of the land of Egypt, afterward destroyed those who did not believe (Jude 5).

And Christ, addressing his disciples who expressed their wonder at the buildings of the temple, was blunt about the future of the pinnacle of Judaism:

> You see all these, [that is, the buildings of the temple] do you not? Truly, I say to you, there will not be left here one stone upon another that will not be thrown down (Matt. 24:2).

Such is a very brief outline of Israel's track record. One word summarises it: disaster!

Take one example of a new-covenant writer making telling use of Israel's history; that is, Israel's history of failure under its covenant:

> As the Holy Spirit says [to us today, that is]: 'Today, if you hear his voice, do not harden your hearts as in the rebellion [of the people of Israel], on the day of testing in the wilderness, where your fathers put me to the test and saw my works for forty years. Therefore I was provoked with that generation, and said: "They always go astray in their heart; they have not known my ways". As I swore in my wrath: "They shall not enter my rest"' (Heb. 3:7-11).

---

[5] Probably better 'Jesus', meaning 'the Lord'.

That's the history of Israel. Now the application – to believers in the first century, and to believers now:

> Take care, brothers, lest there be in any of you an evil, unbelieving heart, leading you to fall away from the living God. But exhort one another every day, as long as it is called 'today', that none of you may be hardened by the deceitfulness of sin. For we have come to share in Christ, if indeed we hold our original confidence firm to the end. As it is said: 'Today, if you hear his voice, do not harden your hearts as in the rebellion'.
>
> Therefore, while the promise of entering his rest still stands, let us fear lest any of you should seem to have failed to reach it. For good news came to us just as to them, but the message they heard did not benefit them, because they were not united by faith with those who listened. For we who have believed enter that rest, as he has said: 'As I swore in my wrath: "They shall not enter my rest"', although his works were finished from the foundation of the world. For he has somewhere spoken of the seventh day in this way: 'And God rested on the seventh day from all his works'. And again in this passage he said: 'They shall not enter my rest'.
>
> Since therefore it remains for some to enter it, and those who formerly received the good news failed to enter because of disobedience, again he appoints a certain day, 'Today', saying through David so long afterward, in the words already quoted: 'Today, if you hear his voice, do not harden your hearts'. For if Joshua had given them rest, God would not have spoken of another day later on. So then, there remains a sabbath rest for the people of God, for whoever has entered God's rest has also rested from his works as God did from his.
>
> Let us therefore strive to enter that rest, so that no one may fall by the same sort of disobedience. For the word of God is living and active, sharper than any two-edged sword, piercing to the division of soul and of spirit, of joints and of marrow, and discerning the thoughts and intentions of the heart. And no creature is hidden from his sight, but all are naked and exposed to the eyes of him to whom we must give account (Heb. 3:12 – 4:13).

* * *

This leaves us with the question, the decision. In light of the above, what is your verdict? Would you say that Israel's history was one of Triumph or Tragedy? Of course, it wasn't either/or, black or white. Nevertheless which of the two would best fit the bill? And what bearing does this have on what we might expect in 'these last days'? I ask this, even though the new covenant is the age of the Spirit, and every believer is indwelt by the Spirit. Despite these signal changes and unspeakable advantages, as we have seen, the New Testament is explicit that Israel's history serves as a warning to us in the days of the new covenant. At the very least, we have to say that it is all too easy for believers to fail under their covenant, and do so just as easily as Israel failed in the days of their covenant. To accommodate the words of Joseph Hart: 'Brethren let us be not too secure'.[6]

---

[6] Joseph Hart's hymn: 'Let us ask the important question'.

The Future:
What Did Christ Predict?

Reader, you might be thinking that this chapter should have come much earlier, even very close to the start. Indeed, I have considered moving it forward. But I have decided to leave it where it stands. It takes us back to the time before the crucifixion, before Pentecost and the establishment of the *ekklēsia*, before the *pseudadelphoi* came on the scene, and well before Christendom and all its conundrums were thought of. It gives us, as it were, an eagle-eye's view of the age from Pentecost until the end of time at the second coming of Christ. Now a great deal of history has been lived since Christ said these things to the first believers – 2000 years' worth, in fact – and when we come to glance at that long history, Christ's predictions must govern our understanding and interpretation of it.

And that is why I have left this chapter where it is.

* * *

I might major on Matthew 24, but I do not. Although I will glance at that chapter, I want to concentrate on Matthew 13 – Christ's parables of the kingdom; namely, the parables of the Sower, the Weeds, the Mustard Seed, the Leaven and the Net. What do these parables tell us about what we should expect in the unfolding history of the *ekklēsia*, the gospel, the work of Christ in the world?

Without majoring on Matthew 24, thus avoiding the need to enter the minefield of its detailed prophetical-interpretation, that chapter is surely of high significance in this debate. I cannot see how anybody can read the chapter and come away confident that this age will be marked by growing triumph. I agree that we have this statement:

The Future: What Did Christ Predict?

This gospel of the kingdom will be proclaimed throughout the whole world (Matt. 24:14).

But look at the rest! Of the time following Christ's crucifixion until his re-appearing, we read:

> See that no one leads you astray. For many will come in my name, saying: 'I am the Christ', and they will lead many astray. And you will hear of wars and rumours of wars. See that you are not alarmed, for this must take place, but the end is not yet. For nation will rise against nation, and kingdom against kingdom, and there will be famines and earthquakes in various places. All these are but the beginning of the birth pains.
> Then they will deliver you up to tribulation and put you to death, and you will be hated by all nations for my name's sake. And then many will fall away and betray one another and hate one another. And many false prophets will arise and lead many astray. And because lawlessness will be increased, the love of many will grow cold. But the one who endures to the end will be saved. And this gospel of the kingdom will be proclaimed throughout the whole world as a testimony to all nations, and then the end will come.
> So when you see the abomination of desolation spoken of by the prophet Daniel, standing in the holy place (let the reader understand), then let those who are in Judea flee to the mountains. Let the one who is on the housetop not go down to take what is in his house, and let the one who is in the field not turn back to take his cloak. And alas for women who are pregnant and for those who are nursing infants in those days! Pray that your flight may not be in winter or on a sabbath. For then there will be great tribulation, such as has not been from the beginning of the world until now, no, and never will be. And if those days had not been cut short, no human being would be saved. But for the sake of the elect those days will be cut short. Then if anyone says to you: 'Look, here is the Christ!' or 'There he is!' do not believe it. For false christs and false prophets will arise and perform great signs and wonders, so as to lead astray, if possible, even the elect. See, I have told you beforehand. So, if they say to you: 'Look, he is in the wilderness', do not go out. If they say: 'Look, he is in the inner rooms', do not believe it. For as the lightning comes from the east and shines as far as the west, so will be the

coming of the Son of Man. Wherever the corpse is, there the vultures will gather.
Immediately after the tribulation of those days the sun will be darkened, and the moon will not give its light, and the stars will fall from heaven, and the powers of the heavens will be shaken. Then will appear in heaven the sign of the Son of Man, and then all the tribes of the earth will mourn, and they will see the Son of Man coming on the clouds of heaven with power and great glory. And he will send out his angels with a loud trumpet call, and they will gather his elect from the four winds, from one end of heaven to the other (Matt. 24:4-31).

If any reader thinks that passage spells a time of growing triumph for the *ekklēsia*, then nothing I can say can possibly bring about a change of opinion. But as I read the chapter, the overall picture is one of tragedy – in the sense of suffering saints, deceptive teachers, false gospels, tribulation, mourning, and so on.

But let me get to my main passage – Matthew 13 – and the parables.

* * *

The Parable of the Sower

A sower went out to sow. And as he sowed, some seeds fell along the path, and the birds came and devoured them. Other seeds fell on rocky ground, where they did not have much soil, and immediately they sprang up, since they had no depth of soil, but when the sun rose they were scorched. And since they had no root, they withered away. Other seeds fell among thorns, and the thorns grew up and choked them. Other seeds fell on good soil and produced grain, some a hundredfold, some sixty, some thirty. He who has ears, let him hear (Matt. 13:3-9).

Christ's Explanation of the Sower

Hear then the parable of the sower: When anyone hears the word of the kingdom and does not understand it, the evil one comes and snatches away what has been sown in his heart. This is what was sown along the path. As for what was sown on rocky ground, this is the one who hears the word and immediately receives it with joy, yet he has no root in himself, but endures for a while, and when tribulation or persecution arises on account of the word, immediately he falls away. As for what was sown among thorns, this is the one who hears the word, but the cares of the world and the deceitfulness of riches choke the word, and it proves unfruitful. As for what was sown on good soil, this is the one who hears the word and understands it. He indeed bears fruit and yields, in one case a hundredfold, in another sixty, and in another thirty (Matt. 13:18-23).

* * *

The Parable of the Weeds

The kingdom of heaven may be compared to a man who sowed good seed in his field, but while his men were sleeping, his enemy came and sowed weeds among the wheat and went away. So when the plants came up and bore grain, then the weeds appeared also. And the servants of the master of the house came and said to him: 'Master, did you not sow good seed in your field? How then does it have weeds?' He said to them: 'An enemy has done this'. So the servants said to him: 'Then do you want us to go and gather them?' But he said: 'No, lest in gathering the weeds you root up the wheat along with them. Let both grow together until the harvest, and at harvest time I will tell the reapers: "Gather the weeds first and bind them in bundles to be burned, but gather the wheat into my barn"' (Matt. 13:24-30).

Christ's Explanation of the Weeds

The one who sows the good seed is the Son of Man. The field is the world, and the good seed is the sons of the kingdom. The weeds are the sons of the evil one, and the enemy who showed them is the devil. The harvest is the end of the age, and the reapers are angels. Just as the weeds are gathered and burned with fire, so will it be at the end of the age. The Son of Man will send his angels, and they will gather out of his kingdom all causes of sin and all law-breakers, and throw them into the fiery furnace. In that place there will be weeping and gnashing of teeth. Then the righteous will shine like the sun in the kingdom of their Father. He who has ears, let him hear (Matt. 13:37-43).

*   *   *

The Parable of the Mustard Seed

> The kingdom of heaven is like a grain of mustard seed that a man took and sowed in his field. It is the smallest of all seeds, but when it has grown it is larger than all the garden plants and becomes a tree, so that the birds of the air come and make nests in its branches (Matt. 13:31-32).

The Parable of the Leaven

> The kingdom of heaven is like leaven that a woman took and hid in three measures of flour, till it was all leavened (Matt. 13:33).

The Parable of the Net

> Again, the kingdom of heaven is like a net that was thrown into the sea and gathered fish of every kind. When it was full, men drew it ashore and sat down and sorted the good into containers but threw away the bad. So it will be at the end of the age. The angels will come out and separate the evil from the righteous and throw them into the fiery furnace. In that place there will be weeping and gnashing of teeth (Matt. 13:47-50).

*   *   *

First things first: these parables are 'kingdom parables'; they concern 'the kingdom of heaven'. This designation is unique to Matthew: the Bible generally speaks of 'the kingdom of God'. Are these two the same? That is one question – to which different answers are given.

Another question: whether we are talking about 'the kingdom of heaven' or 'the kingdom of God', what is 'the kingdom'? Opinions, again, are divided.

Simplistic this may be, but I am taking 'the kingdom of heaven' and 'the kingdom of God' to speak of God's spiritual reign in this age *as it seems to us*. In other words, I take these parables to be Christ's description of the progress of what purports to be, and what is seen to be, what we think to be, God's spiritual rule during this present age.

To simplify matters still further, I think that Christ here tells us in parable form what we are to expect of the gospel, the *ekklēsia* – or as it is far more commonly known now, during the reign of Christendom – the church, Christianity (if you will) during the time between Pentecost and the return of Christ.

* * *

We learn, first of all, that Christ predicted that during this age there will a great deal of spiritual activity: sowing, whether the sowing of good seed – the word of God – or the sowing of bad seed – weeds, error, falsehood; kneading of dough; fishing, catching both good and bad fish in the net. Activity is the word!

Growth, expansion, will be another mark of this time. The sowing of seed leads to a harvest with its consequent multiplication of grain; leaven expands and spreads throughout the entire batch of dough; the mustard seed dies in the ground but develops into a great tree. Growth, expansion will mark this age.

But while the parables speak of activity and expansion, do they speak of triumph or tragedy for the gospel? Which best describes the overall picture?

True, there will be a good harvest with an ingathering of wholesome grain; some good fish will be caught in the net; and so on. But the overall picture is far from rosy. It is, at best, mixed. If I can use such a term, very mixed. The sower scatters his seed, and while some lands on good soil, much is lost on the wayside, on the rocky ground or among thorns. The field is sown with good seed, but the enemy sows weeds. The net lands good fish, but also bad. And while the growth of a great tree from the mustard seed, and the fermentation of the leaven, are often taken to speak of a glorious spiritual growth during this age, Scripture uses both images to speak of evil. Moreover, as

The Future: What Did Christ Predict?

Christ explained, the birds (Matt. 13:4) represent 'the evil one' (Matt. 13:19); or his agents.

As for leaven, we know that in preparation for the Passover:

> ...the people of Israel were required to go through their houses and remove every trace of leaven (Ex. 12:15-39; 13:3,7).

And the illustration is carried over into the new covenant; Paul, writing to the Corinthians was dogmatic:

> Your boasting is not good. Do you not know that a little leaven leavens the whole lump? Cleanse out the old leaven that you may be a new lump, as you really are unleavened. For Christ, our Passover lamb, has been sacrificed. Let us therefore celebrate the festival, not with the old leaven, the leaven of malice and evil, but with the unleavened bread of sincerity and truth (1 Cor. 5:6-8).

As he said to the Galatians:

> You were running well. Who hindered you from obeying the truth? This persuasion is not from him who calls you. A little leaven leavens the whole lump (Gal. 5:7-9).

As Christ himself had made clear, and repeatedly so:

> 'Watch and beware of the leaven of the Pharisees and Sadducees... How is it that you fail to understand that I did not speak about bread? Beware of the leaven of the Pharisees and Sadducees'. Then they understood that he did not tell them to beware of the leaven of bread, but of the teaching of the Pharisees and Sadducees (Matt. 16:6,11-12).

Again:

> Beware of the leaven of the Pharisees, which is hypocrisy (Luke 12:1).

And again:

> Watch out; beware of the leaven of the Pharisees and the leaven of Herod (Mark 8:15).

In the old covenant, leaven was forbidden in sacrifices (Ex. 23:18; 34:25; Lev. 2:11; 6:17; 10:12; Deut. 16:3-4). It could be

75

used (Lev. 7:13; 23:17; Amos 4:5), but not on the altar (Lev. 2:11).

The position is clear: 'leaven', in Scripture, generally stands for evil.

As for the way Scripture uses the image of the 'tree', two Old Testament passages surely form the backdrop to Christ's use of the image in the parable; I refer to Nebuchadnezzar's vision of God's judgment upon him (Dan. 4:10-26), and Ezekiel's use of the tree to illustrate God's wrath against Assyria then Egypt (Ezek. 31:3-18):

Here is Daniel's interpretation of the king's vision:

> My lord, may the dream be for those who hate you and its interpretation for your enemies! The tree you saw, which grew and became strong, so that its top reached to heaven, and it was visible to the end of the whole earth, whose leaves were beautiful and its fruit abundant, and in which was food for all, under which beasts of the field found shade, and in whose branches the birds of the heavens lived – it is you, O king, who have grown and become strong. Your greatness has grown and reaches to heaven, and your dominion to the ends of the earth. And because the king saw a watcher, a holy one, coming down from heaven and saying: 'Chop down the tree and destroy it, but leave the stump of its roots in the earth, bound with a band of iron and bronze, in the tender grass of the field, and let him be wet with the dew of heaven, and let his portion be with the beasts of the field, till seven periods of time pass over him', this is the interpretation, O king: It is a decree of the Most High, which has come upon my lord the king, that you shall be driven from among men, and your dwelling shall be with the beasts of the field. You shall be made to eat grass like an ox, and you shall be wet with the dew of heaven, and seven periods of time shall pass over you, till you know that the Most High rules the kingdom of men and gives it to whom he will. And as it was commanded to leave the stump of the roots of the tree, your kingdom shall be confirmed for you from the time that you know that heaven rules. Therefore, O king, let my counsel be acceptable to you: break off your sins by practicing righteousness, and your

iniquities by showing mercy to the oppressed, that there may perhaps be a lengthening of your prosperity (Dan. 4:19-27).

And here is God's interpretation, (through Ezekiel) of the vision of the tree:

> Because it [the tree, that is Assyria, then Egypt] towered high and set its top among the clouds, and its heart was proud of its height, I will give it into the hand of a mighty one of the nations. He shall surely deal with it as its wickedness deserves. I have cast it out. Foreigners, the most ruthless of nations, have cut it down and left it. On the mountains and in all the valleys its branches have fallen, and its boughs have been broken in all the ravines of the land, and all the peoples of the earth have gone away from its shadow and left it. On its fallen trunk dwell all the birds of the heavens, and on its branches are all the beasts of the field. All this is in order that no trees by the waters may grow to towering height or set their tops among the clouds, and that no trees that drink water may reach up to them in height. For they are all given over to death, to the world below, among the children of man, with those who go down to the pit...
>
> On the day the cedar went down to Sheol I caused mourning; I closed the deep over it, and restrained its rivers, and many waters were stopped. I clothed Lebanon in gloom for it, and all the trees of the field fainted because of it. I made the nations quake at the sound of its fall, when I cast it down to Sheol with those who go down to the pit. And all the trees of Eden, the choice and best of Lebanon, all that drink water, were comforted in the world below. They also went down to Sheol with it, to those who are slain by the sword; yes, those who were its arm, who lived under its shadow among the nations.
>
> Whom are you thus like in glory and in greatness among the trees of Eden? You shall be brought down with the trees of Eden to the world below. You shall lie among the uncircumcised, with those who are slain by the sword. This is Pharaoh and all his multitude (Ezek. 31:10-18).

As can be seen, neither passage speaks of the triumph of a kingdom; quite the reverse. Expansion, growth, yes, but definitely evil.

* * *

The Future: What Did Christ Predict?

Well, there it is. What we have to decide is whether or not what I have called 'the seeming work of God' during this age, is, according to Christ, going to be marked by Triumph or Tragedy? There will be much labour, much growth, much expansion, much seeming success, but will the overall result be good or bad? As before, it is not either/or; nevertheless, the picture Christ has painted is not altogether pleasant – it clearly does not lend itself to triumphalism.

The Past 2000 Years

Having already written extensively on what I have called 'the seeming work of God' during the period from Pentecost to the rise of the Separatists,[1] and having already said something about it in this book, in this chapter I will sketch only the briefest of outlines of the past two millennia, marking out what, in light of what we have so far discovered, I see as the significant turning points in the history. I stress that what follows is only a brief outline of a very complicated story.[2] I am speaking of Christendom's Rise, Christendom's Reign, Christendom Tinkered With, Christendom's Flourishing, and Christendom's Demise. In particular, I have the West in mind.

Christendom's Rise

I speak of Christendom. What do I mean by it? I am referring to what happened in the time of the Fathers (roughly the second to the fifth centuries). By 'the Fathers', I mean those theological politicians who adulterated the new covenant, the *ekklēsia*, in particular, by making the old covenant the norm and pattern for the new, thus directly contradicting Christ's teaching in his parable of the wineskins (Matt. 9:16-17) and the events at the Passover meal in the upper room (John 13 – 17).[3] They also adopted pagan ideas into their system. In short, I am speaking of those men who replaced the new-covenant revelation with a Judaised-paganised Christianity, supplanting the dominant and vital role of the Spirit with a legal religion. This took a fatal turn when the Roman emperors got involved. Under Diocletian (284-305), believers had suffered horrendous persecution, but with the so-called conversion of Constantine (324-337), followed by the reign of Theodosius I (379-392; 392-395),

---

[1] See my *Battle*.
[2] For far more, see Stuart Murray: *Post-Christendom*, Paternoster, Carlisle, 2004.
[3] See my *The Upper Room*.

Christianity (patristic-style) became the State Religion of the Empire. The political/religious conglomerate known as Christendom had been formed.[4] A Judaised-paganised Christianity, enforced by Roman law, had now became the norm.[5] Dissension spelled 'heresy'.

Let me summarise some of the consequences of Christendom within the *ekklēsia*: the establishment or confirmation of the laity/clergy split, the imposition of a hierarchy, the virtual elimination of the priesthood of all believers – replacing it with priestcraft, the absolute dominance of the monologue sermon – sacramentalism, sacerdotalism, the vicious persecution of nonconformist believers,[6] infant sprinkling with baptismal regeneration, the erection of sacred buildings, and the like. Disastrous!

More was to come, and quickly! Within a very short time, this formation of Christendom led to the emergence of the Bishop of Rome as the top dog of the religious half of the monstrosity. As for the political supremo, that depended on the rise and fall of empires and kingdoms in the various states where Christendom inexorably spread it grasping tentacles. But two masters in one house was always bound to be unstable. And so it proved: the bitter tension was endlessly played out as the Pope and the King (or Emperor) fought for mastery; first one, then the other, held the whip hand. Meanwhile the vast majority of the *hoi polloi* were born, lived (existed) and died in abject

---

[4] See my *The Pastor*; *Infant*; *Battle*; Appendix 1 'Christendom' in my *Relationship*.
[5] See Appendix 4.
[6] I do not use the term here in the narrow sense of the 15th-century Separatists and others who refused to conform to the Church of England. I am speaking of those who refuse allegiance to the institutions of Christendom. In the early days, the Donatists; later, the Albigenses and Waldensians, Lollards and Hussites, Anabaptists, and so on. See E.H.Broadbent: *The Pilgrim Church*, Pickering and Inglis, London, 1935; Leonard Verduin: *The Reformers and Their Stepchildren*, The Paternoster Press, Exeter, 1964; reprinted, Baker Book House, Grand Rapids, 1980.

darkness and delusion, 'comforted' only by the thought that their sprinkling as a baby by a duly ordained priest, and the mystical ministrations of that priest throughout their life and beyond, would get them 'right with God'. Or so they vainly hoped, trusting that what their priests told them was the truth.

Christendom's Reign

I am speaking of the Dark Ages (roughly 500-1500). I do not use this term to give the impression that there was no progress in terms of scientific invention, education, mathematics, astronomy and the like. Of course not. But spiritually speaking, the term is an apt description of the time. Christendom ruled: in the West, Roman Christendom ruled; in the East, Greek (with a subdivision, Russian). And the delusion and darkness of the general population continued unabated as priestcraft maintained its iron grip. Voices of protest were raised.[7] But...

Christendom Tinkered With

Although there were earlier protestors against the widespread Christendom-corruption, it was only in the early 16th-century that Martin Luther, with his ninety-five theses at Wittenberg, really kick-started the Reformation. The outcome of that stupendous upheaval was a huge split in Christendom. From that time on, Western Christendom was divided into Roman Christendom and Reformed (Evangelical) Christendom.[8] Some radicals – mainly Anabaptists – tried to break free of the shackles of Christendom, and as a result, were forced to face cruel Christendom-persecution from both wings, the Roman and the Reformed. The upshot was that Christendom continued in its two forms – Roman and Reformed – with what seemed a minuscule minority of believers who rejected the monstrosity's claims. As for the overall effect of the Reformation, while the

---

[7] See the 'The Long Night' in my *New-Covenant Articles Volume Six*.
[8] What about Lutheranism? In many respects, Luther did not really break from Rome, and the subsequent history of Lutheranism bears this out.

Reformed wing certainly recovered scriptural ground on soteriology, alas, it left Christendom intact as far as the *ekklēsia* was concerned; infant baptism retained its dominant grip, and although presbytercraft replaced priestcraft, the Reformation left the fundamental clergy/laity structure unaltered. As John Milton put it, the new presbyter was simply the old priest 'writ large'. The 'faithful' were still largely spectators who attended 'a place of worship' – that is, 'went to church' – at specified 'times of worship', where they watched and heard, not a priest offering a sacrifice (as they continued to do in Roman Christendom), but a minister preaching a sermon. In both branches of Western Christendom, Reformed as well as Roman, the so-called laity remained a lower order than the clergy; it was the clergy who continued to pull the levers of power as they performed – I use the word advisedly – their appointed duties. I am not saying no good was done in the years which followed the Reformation, but the Reformation did not annihilate all the evils of Christendom. Far from it! Some Christendom-distortions of the new covenant were actually entrenched![9]

Christendom's Flourishing

In the years following the Reformation, one feature stands out. It almost goes without saying that false teachers and their teaching have never abated during all these long years since Pentecost, but the issue I want to highlight now is the way in which believers – for many years – have been so conditioned to regard Christendom as the biblical norm that they have been prepared to adopt Christendom-principles[10] and, on that basis, modify – 're-engineer' is the buzz word – the *ekklēsia* to fit what has become the overriding aim: to adjust the *ekklēsia* and the gospel it preaches to meet the whims of pagans in order to attract those pagans into church attendance. It goes without

---

[9] For Stephen K.Ray's taunts, see Ray pp43-49.

[10] Fundamentally, that believers – including evangelicals, not just Rome – have tacitly accept the concept of 'development'. See the earlier notes on Newman.

saying that, since the Reformation, apart from the early Separatists, and a few radicals who have erupted from time to time, getting unbelievers to attend a place of preaching and listen to a sermon has been the staple means of evangelism – both evangelical, in general, and Reformed, in particular.[11] But this past fifty years, this has gone into over-drive. As I say, the *ekklēsia* has been so modified that its number-one priority is rapidly becoming the attraction of pagans into church attendance. Consequently, the *ekklēsia* has adopted the features of being just another global business, a virtual market-place.[12] As a result, the *ekklēsia* (sadly, even among Separatists) is becoming a mixed regenerate and unregenerate multitude, where the scriptural separation of the *ekklēsia* and the world has all but broken down.[13] Take the Lord's supper. The concept of 'a closed table' is becoming virtually unknown – certainly, unappreciated, unwelcome – in evangelical circles. The Lord's supper is commonly part of the public work of the *ekklēsia*, with scant – if any – serious warning given – this warning, even when it is given, washing over the heads of most; discipline at the supper is rapidly breaking down. The direction of travel for the *ekklēsia* is directly away from its new-covenant norm – secret, private, for the mutual edification of the saints – into a public performance geared to social-media distribution.[14] Christendom has grabbed the internet with both hands. So much so, it will not be long before no believer will be alive

---

[11] D.Martyn Lloyd-Jones has had a big contemporary influence in this area. As John Brencher rightly observed, Lloyd-Jones' conviction was 'that evangelism, in effect, was completely tied in to the set-piece sermon and people were expected to attend the services and hear the word' (John Brencher: *Martyn Lloyd-Jones (1899-1981) and Twentieth-Century Evangelicalism*, Paternoster Press, Carlisle, 2002, p187). In more recent times, however, while 'the set-piece sermon' is still a feature of most 'church services', the modern adjusted-*ekklēsia* offers a far wider selection of attractions, attractions which have a far-wider appeal to pagans.

[12] See my *Attracting*.

[13] Many of my works have been taken up with this theme. See my latest: *The Upper Room*.

[14] See my *Church*; *Public*.

who knew what Christianity was before the dawn and dominance of the electronic age. Hence my use of 'flourishing' in the heading for this section – not the flourishing of the *ekklēsia*, but the flourishing of Christendom-churchianity as it adapts to each new development of the digital means of the dissemination of information. In order to function today, an evangelical church needs a growing band of tech-savvy professionals – whizz-kids – to manage a bewildering array of IT apparatus. Many believers are absolutely hooked on endlessly hearing or watching monologue sermons from their favourite preacher. Little else seems to matter. The concept of the priesthood of all believers is fading – if it has not already faded – into oblivion.

Post-Christendom

Whole books have been written on post-Christendom.[15] I confine my brief remarks to the UK. I could extend this to include the USA, because from what I hear and read of events across the Atlantic, as I write (early 2024) this presidential-election year provides almost daily evidence of an upsurge of Christendom with, for instance, evangelical talk of Donald Trump as some kind of reincarnation of Cyrus, with the United States as a second Judah. As I see it, these evangelicals are repeating the fundamental Christendom-mistake, and imposing the Old Testament – the old covenant for Israel – on their nation. And this, it goes without saying, runs directly contrary to the principles of the Founding Fathers in establishing the American constitution. For an increasing number of American evangelicals, the separation of Church and State is well down the road to becoming a museum piece.

But I confine my remarks to the UK.

There can be little – if any – doubt that since the 1960s, Christendom has been losing its grip on UK society. I am not

---

[15] I have already referred to Stuart Murray: *Post-Christendom*, Paternoster, Carlisle, 2004.

saying Christendom is dead – there's plenty of it all around us in buildings, State flummery, novels, and the like – but the evidence is far too strong to be gainsaid: Christendom's grip is weakening. Ignorance of the basic elements of the gospel is common, and growing. 'Christian-observance' – however defined – is terminally-weakening across the board.

But I want to make – and stress – a point of the utmost importance: I acknowledge the post-Christendom phenomenon in society, but, contrary to most evangelicals, I actually welcome this. But even if I did not go this far, the issue I want to stress is this: in this book – indeed, in my life and ministry – it is not the state of society which fundamentally bothers me; it is the state of the *ekklēsia*. And this is because it is precisely the concern I find in the post-Pentecost Scriptures. While Christendom is fast losing its grip on UK society, it maintains a velvet-gloved iron-grip on most believers. In 'Christian circles', in the thinking of most believers, Christendom is as much alive as ever it was;[16] most evangelicals even inadvertently use the advent of post-Christendom in society to enforce Christendom's grip on the *ekklēsia*. Perhaps I should put it the other way about: Christendom moves believers to use post-Christendom principles to enforce Christendom on the *ekklēsia*![17] In other words, things are getting far worse, in a fundamental sense, not better.

* * *

Well, that's my take on the effect of Christendom. You may not agree. If so, how do you view things? How does your view stack up with Scripture?

And if you broadly agree with what I have set out, you must realise that this leaves us with the question, the decision. In light of the above, what is your verdict? Would you say that the course of the gospel during this age since Pentecost has been

---

[16] It is just that most believers don't recognise it.
[17] Sideline truth, count the popularity, sell the books in quantity, press 'donate', bank the bucks.

one of Triumph or Tragedy? Of course, it's not either/or, black or white. Nevertheless which of the two would best fit the bill?

OBJECTIONS

Objections

From time to time, I have been asking you, reader, how you would sum up what I have described as 'the seeming work of God' this past 2000 years. It is pretty obvious what my view is – more of a tragedy than a triumph. And I think the evidence I have offered is convincing.

Wait a minute, says the objector. All this is very fine, but...

In this chapter, I want to examine some common objections made against my thesis,[1] objections made on the basis of Scripture.

Objection 1

Since Christ promised:

> I will build my church, and the gates of hell shall not prevail against it (Matt. 16:18)...

...can we not expect to see the church advancing, growing, conquering, triumphant throughout this age?

Let us pause and take stock. Clearly, Christ used an illustration – city gates – when he says that 'the gates of hell [Hades, death]' will not prevail against the church (the *ekklēsia*). Hades, as I have indicated, means death. Death will never be able to prevent the *ekklēsia* from carrying out its ministry. And the principal part of that ministry is to enable believers to edify each other (Rom. 12:3-8; 15:14; 1 Cor. 1:4-7; 12:4-31; 14:1-40; Gal. 6:1-2,10; Eph. 4:1-16; 1 Thess. 5:11,14; Heb. 10:24-25; 1 Pet. 2:2-5; 4:10-11; Jude 20-23, for instance),[2] and promote their mutual transformation by the Spirit into Christ's likeness (Rom. 8:28-30; 12:2; 2 Cor. 3:17-18; Eph. 4:12-16; Phil. 3:10;

---

[1] I say 'my thesis' only in the sense that this is my conviction, that which I have put forward in this book. I do not, for a moment, pretend that I invented this view, or that I am the only one to hold it.
[2] See my *The Priesthood*.

Objections

Col. 3:10; 1 John 2:6; 4:17). Death will not be able to stop that; death will not have the last word. Indeed, there is more: the *ekklēsia* will be used of God to preach the gospel, in the fullest sense of the word 'preach' – both publicly and privately (Acts 20:20) – as the means whereby sinners (that is, elect sinners) might be saved (1 Cor. 1:17-18; 2 Cor. 5:19 – 6:2, for instance) and thus released from the grip and dominion of death. And Christ meant 'death' both physically and spiritually.[3]

Christ was not promising that the *ekklēsia* will be a massive, conquering power in the world; rather, it will never be stopped in its God-determined purpose for saints and sinners. God will always maintain the gospel through the *ekklēsia*, whatever Satanic defences are set up against it. Hades, death, will not be able to hold the elect in its grip.

This is true physically. Christ, the firstfruits (1 Cor. 15:20) rose from the dead; that is, he rose physically from the dead. Christ died, yes, but death could not hold him. As Robert Lowry put it:

> *Death cannot keep his prey.*
> *Jesus, my Saviour!*
> *He tore the bars away,*
> *Jesus my Lord!*

Consequently, as Paul argued, and argued at length, believers, individually, are certain to rise from the dead, rise physically (1

---

[3] A city without gates is unprotected, and easily plundered. Take God's prophecy against Kedar and Hazor: 'A nation at ease, that dwells securely, declares the LORD, that has no gates or bars, that dwells alone. Their camels shall become plunder, their herds of livestock a spoil. I will scatter to every wind those who cut the corners of their hair, and I will bring their calamity from every side of them, declares the LORD' (Jer. 49:31-32). Again, God's prophecy against Gog: 'You will devise an evil scheme and say: "I will go up against the land of un-walled villages. I will fall upon the quiet people who dwell securely, all of them dwelling without walls, and having no bars or gates", to seize spoil and carry off plunder' (Ezek. 38:10-12). See also Deut. 3:5; Zech. 2:4.

Objections

Cor. 15). Death's gates will not be able to maintain its grip on the dead.

But Christ's promise extends to spiritual death as well as to physical death.

Believers, like all men (Eph. 2:1-3), were born dead in sins, dead spiritually. But, when they are regenerated by the Spirit (John 1:11-13; 3:3-8; Jas. 1:18; 1 Pet. 1:2-3,23), they repent and trust the Redeemer – they pass from death to life:

> Truly, truly, I say to you, whoever hears my word and believes him who sent me has eternal life. He does not come into judgment, but has passed from death to life (John 5:24).
>
> We know that we have passed out of death into life (1 John 3:14).

Hades, death, cannot hold the elect spiritually.[4] The Spirit is far too strong for the gates of Hades to keep the elect captive.

As Christ, linking the spiritual and the physical, made clear:

> Truly, truly, I say to you, an hour is coming, and is now here, when the dead will hear the voice of the Son of God, and those who hear will live. For as the Father has life in himself, so he has granted the Son also to have life in himself. And he has given him authority to execute judgment, because he is the Son of Man. Do not marvel at this, for an hour is coming when all who are in the tombs will hear his voice and come out, those who have done good to the resurrection of life, and those who have done evil to the resurrection of judgment (John 5:25-29).

And all is in Christ. As Isaac Watts expressed it:

> *Jesus, we bless your Father's name;*
> *Your God and ours are both the same;*
> *What heav'nly blessings from his throne*
> *Flow down to sinners through his Son!*

---

[4] See Kevin DeYoung: 'A Closer Look at the Gates of Hell' (Gospel Coalition).

Objections

> *'Christ be my first elect', he said,*
> *Then chose our souls in Christ our head,*
> *Before he gave the mountains birth...*

In short, Matthew 16:18 does not tell us that the *ekklēsia* will become a triumphant world-power. Rather, it is Christ's categorical assurance that the devil and all the hosts of hell will not be able to withstand the Spirit's edification of the saints, nor his power to call sinners by the gospel. The elect will hear the word, they will heed it, and the elect – every last one of them – will be saved. And in the last day, every one of the elect will be raised from the dead physically to enter Christ's everlasting kingdom at his appearing. Christ's promise in Matthew 16:18 has nothing to do with any millennial kingdom.

Objection 2

Since Christ promised:

> I am with you always, to the end of the age (Matt. 28:20)...

...and since Christ always keeps his promise, surely this must mean that my thesis must be wrong.

Not at all! Christ, of course, always keeps his promise: 'I am with you always, to the end of the age' (Matt. 28:20), but this does not mean that the *ekklēsia* will never be invaded, that false teachers will not infiltrate themselves into the *ekklēsia*, that absolutely pristine, holiness and discipline will always be maintained in the *ekklēsia* throughout the age. Glance again at what we have seen of the early days of the new covenant. But, notwithstanding all the failures, mistakes – and, even sins – along the way, Christ is always with, in and among his true disciples, he will preserve and edify his saints, and all the elect will be saved. Christ will ensure it; as he made clear:

> This is the will of him who sent me, that I should lose nothing of all that he has given me, but raise it up on the last day. For this is the will of my Father, that everyone who looks on the Son and believes in him should have eternal life, and I will raise him up on the last day (John 6:39-40).

Objections

In particular, of his earthly ministry, as he said to his Father in prayer:

> I have manifested your name to the people whom you gave me out of the world. Yours they were, and you gave them to me, and they have kept your word... While I was with them, I kept them in your name, which you have given me. I have guarded them, and not one of them has been lost except the son of destruction, that the Scripture might be fulfilled. But now I am coming to you, and these things I speak in the world, that they may have my joy fulfilled in themselves. I have given them your word, and the world has hated them because they are not of the world, just as I am not of the world. I do not ask that you take them out of the world, but that you keep them from the evil one. They are not of the world, just as I am not of the world (John 17:6,12-16; see John 18:8-9).

And this applies no less to his present mediatorial ministry (Rom. 8:34; Heb. 7:25; 9:24). Christ's promise ensures it:

> All authority in heaven and on earth has been given to me. Go therefore and make disciples of all nations, baptising them in the name of the Father and of the Son and of the Holy Spirit, teaching them to observe all that I have commanded you. And behold, I am with you always, to the end of the age (Matt. 28:18-20).

But as far as false teachers (touting their false gospel) are concerned, Matthew 28:20 does not mean that the *ekklēsia* will always keeps itself clear of error. As I have shown, false teachers and their invasion of the *ekklēsia* caused Paul huge sorrow, and much of the letters he wrote is taken up with combating such men and their lies. And we have Christ's rebukes of various assemblies as recorded in Revelation 2 and 3.

Objection 3

But, says an objector, Paul is adamant:

> The church (*ekklēsia*) of the living God [is] a pillar and buttress of the truth (1 Tim. 3:15).

Objections

If – since – this so, runs the objection, how can the history of the *ekklēsia* be dismissed as a tragedy?

But I am not 'dismissing' the *ekklēsia*. Not at all. Nevertheless, I stand by the claim that *Christendom has wreaked havoc on the* ekklēsia, *and given most believers a false impression of what the* ekklēsia *is supposed to be*. Indeed, Christendom has done immense harm to the world's concept of Christ and the gospel. And, after all, we know that what people *perceive* as the truth is, in reality, more important than the truth itself. In other words, most believers (let alone the men of the world) really do imagine that what Christendom presents as the *ekklēsia* really is the *ekklēsia*; for most believers, their local church, the place where they 'worship God', and the people who meet there – give-or-take a few minor hiccoughs – really is what the New Testament means by the *ekklēsia*. And anyone with the temerity (or, as some would say, the audacity, the madness) to question this is automatically written off as a crank[5] or heretic.[6]

In any case, let's look at Paul's assertion. Yes, 'the church of the living God [is] a pillar and buttress of the truth' (1 Tim. 3:15); that is what he wrote. But which church is this? Is it The Reformed Baptist Church in Staunch-Standing-In-The-Marsh, or The Jolly Evangelical Community-Fellowship in Much-Excitement-On-The-Stage, or The Just-Compare-Our-Mall-Specials-Temple (You Have to Taste the Coffee to Believe It!), or The Wobbly Presbyterian Church in Muddle-Over-Edge, or The Fourteenth Ultra Reformed Presbyterian Church of some American metropolis, or The Miniscule Continuing Orthodox 1647 Reformed Church of The Outer Isles? Or is it one of the 'great' denominations? Or is it The Roman Catholic Church?[7]

---

[5] A crank is a person who has strange ideas and behaves in strange ways. Or is considered such. A nutcase, an oddity, an oddball, whacky...

[6] I wonder if you can detect a personal note in this?

[7] Even such an enthusiastic convert as Stephen K.Ray admitted: 'No one claims the [Roman] Catholic Church has been perfect' (Ray p43). Nevertheless, he still maintained that 'the sacred tradition of the [Roman] Catholic Church' is 'the pillar and foundation of the truth'.

Objections

Which Confession shall we take as definitive? Westminster, Heidelberg, Savoy, London, Philadelphia, Rome?

Until we can be given the definitive answer to such questions – and the stubborn fact remains that no such body exists about which we can all be persuaded is 'the church' – I remain unconvinced. And to talk about 'the true church', 'the invisible church', is, as I have argued, nothing but a cop out. We are talking about truth, practical truth, not some abstract, theoretical, ethereal notion of truth. The point is, we need to know – boots on the ground – which church we are talking about *in a real, actual, practical, day-to-day sense*. Where is the church – which for the last 2000 years – has remained 'a pillar and buttress of the truth'? None of the churches of the New Testament, even though most might have been founded by an apostle, fits the bill.

And those who gloss 1 Timothy 3:15 to make it read that 'the church of the living God [should be] a pillar and buttress of the truth' are simply rewriting Scripture in light of experience – the reverse of what evangelicals claim they do! Moreover, they are actually confirming my point for me!

The best I can suggest is to say that the overwhelming version of the truth that this world receives is that which it receives from 'the church'; that is, Christendom. And that, if my thesis is right, shows just how desperate things have become. Even before Christendom was invented, false teachers were infesting the *ekklēsia*, and ruining the gospel. The invention of Christendom – far from countering this tendency – reinforced it, and continues to do so. What a dismal prospect for the world! With rare exceptions, the only gospel they hear and see is Christendom's version! And that thought has given me a sense of urgency in producing this present publication.[8]

'Believers must listen to the Church. The Church will have [that is, has] the power to make decisions that are binding upon... believers', meaning 'the Roman Catholic Church' has that power (Ray pp32-34).
[8] I confess that my suggestion is exceedingly weak. Whether or not Peter had this verse in mind when he wrote 2 Pet. 3:16, I don't know,

Objection 4

Did Paul not claim that God always gave him – and, by extension, gave all preachers, all believers – a triumphant voyage? After all, he clearly stated:

> Thanks be to God, who in Christ always leads us in triumphal procession (2 Cor. 2:14).

Taking up the word 'clearly' – clearly Paul was using an illustration to make his point in his second letter to the Corinthians. Not wishing to extend my book, I simply state that, as the context makes plain,[9] Paul was here dealing with false teachers, the *pseudadelphoi*, the so-called super-apostles, and at this stage in his letter, he has just opened his case against these men and their teaching. Surprising as it may seem, the note he wished to strike was one of weakness. And having raised the subject of weakness, throughout the rest of the letter he can never break free of it, and move on. Of course not; for the apostle, this personal weakness was a major part of his response to the *pseudadelphoi*.[10]

In the illustration, the big picture is clear. There is triumph, certainly. Roman generals, on their return to Rome following a great victory in battle, were favoured with a triumphal procession through the city. And the conquered-slaves – especially the bigwigs among them – were included in the parade in order to enhance the glory of the conqueror-general. They were not there sharing in their conqueror's triumph; they were there to bring glory to the general. He had conquered them. Paul used that picture to illustrate the new-covenant ministry of believers. Christ is the one who is triumphant. That, of course, needs no proof. But what gave Paul comfort was the

---

but it certainly describes my experience. Nevertheless, triumphalists will have their work cut out to find a convincing explanation of the passage.
[9] See my *False*.
[10] I intend to produce a work on this very issue, and leave my full arguments to that time.

Objections

knowledge that believers in their weakness are included Christ's triumphant procession.

But the all-important question is this: where do believers appear in the procession? Are they standing alongside the general in the general's chariot, graciously bowing this way and that, chests puffed, arrogantly granting the royal wave from side to side in acknowledgement of the plaudits of the crowd? Or do they make up the stumbling, bedraggled chain-gang of conquered slaves, mocked by the watching mob, only having a place in the procession as part of the general's treasure and adding to his glory?

The various Scripture versions do not agree where the emphasis should fall.

The KJV, for instance, which historically has wielded such a massive influence – and still does for many[11] – lays it squarely on the believer's triumph:

> Now thanks be unto God, which always causes[12] us to triumph in Christ, and makes[13] manifest the savour of his knowledge by us in every place.

So does the NASB:

> But thanks be to God, who always leads us in triumph in Christ, and through us reveals the fragrance of the knowledge of him in every place.

Both are wrong.

The Christian Standard Bible and the Holman Standard both leave it open.

Other versions, however, get it unequivocally right:

NIV (2011):

---

[11] See, for instance, Peter Masters: 'Dispersing Gloomy Seasons of the Soul (2)'.
[12] Original 'causeth'.
[13] Original 'maketh'.

> But thanks be to God, who always leads us as captives in Christ's triumphal procession and uses us to spread the aroma of the knowledge of him everywhere.

Berean Standard Bible:

> But thanks be to God, who always leads us triumphantly as captives in Christ and through us spreads everywhere the fragrance of the knowledge of him.

New Living Translation:

> But thank God! He has made us his captives and continues to lead us along in Christ's triumphal procession. Now he uses us to spread the knowledge of Christ everywhere, like a sweet perfume.

Good News:

> But thanks be to God! For in union with Christ we are always led by God as prisoners in Christ's victory procession. God uses us to make the knowledge about Christ spread everywhere like a sweet fragrance.

Colossians 2:15 is the only other place where the word *thriambeuō*, 'lead in triumph', is used in Scripture, and it's use in that verse makes the point:

> [Christ] disarmed the rulers and authorities and put them to open shame, by triumphing over them in him.

As Charles Ellicott commented:

> There is absolutely no authority for the factitive meaning [that is, 'causes'] given to the verb in the English [Authorised or King James] version. In Colossians 2:15, it is translated rightly 'triumphing over them in it'. It is obvious, too, that the true rendering gives a much more characteristic thought. It would be unlike... Paul to speak of himself as the triumphant commander of God's great army.

This does not exhaust the illustration. The chained slaves trudging in the procession were, in fact, trudging to their

Objections

slaughter. And that, in order to add to the glory of their conqueror.[14]

Paul brought out his meaning by a second illustration; namely, that of an odour, an aroma, a fragrance – or, not to be squeamish about it – a smell:

> Thanks be to God, who in Christ always leads us in triumphal procession, and through us spreads the fragrance of the knowledge of him everywhere. For we are the aroma of Christ to God among those who are being saved and among those who are perishing, to one a fragrance from death to death, to the other a fragrance from life to life (2 Cor. 2:14-16).

This could be a reference to the pagan offering of incense in that procession. I tend to the view, however, that, as so often with Paul, this a case of where he was never worried about mixing his metaphors, muddling his illustrations. As long as he could drive home his spiritual meaning, literary concerns meant little or nothing to him.[15] Pedantic publishing rules (if there had been any in those days) would have been of no concern – as long as his readers and hearers got the message. (Now *there's* a lesson for all preachers – and Christian writers – today!) Here is a case in point; the apostle moved seamlessly from a Roman procession to the levitical priesthood and the offering of sacrifices. Indeed, the idea of a sweet odour – sweet to God that is, however repugnant the smell might be to man – pre-dates even the old covenant:

> Noah built an altar to the LORD and took some of every clean animal and some of every clean bird and offered burnt offerings on the altar. And... the LORD smelled the pleasing aroma (Gen. 8:20-21).

---

[14] Many disagree, and think that Paul was speaking of his triumph. They include John Calvin, John Gill and John MacArthur.

[15] Take Eph. 4:14-16. Paul tells believers to grow up, not be corks on the sea at the mercy of tide and wind, duped by schemers, so that they can play an active role in the building of a healthy body. Take 1 Thess. 5:1-11. Talking of the second coming of Christ, Paul speaks of the coming of a thief, a woman in labour, staying awake and sober, prepared for battle clothed in armour.

Objections

As for the old covenant itself, references are legion. Here is a sample:

> You shall cut the ram into pieces, and wash its entrails and its legs, and put them with its pieces and its head, and burn the whole ram on the altar. It is a burnt offering to the LORD. It is a pleasing aroma, a food offering to the LORD (Ex. 29:17-18).

> Aaron's sons the priests shall arrange the pieces, the head, and the fat, on the wood that is on the fire on the altar; but its entrails and its legs he shall wash with water. And the priest shall burn all of it on the altar, as a burnt offering, a food offering with a pleasing aroma to the LORD... It is a burnt offering, a food offering with a pleasing aroma to the LORD (Lev. 1:8-9,13).

> When anyone brings a grain offering as an offering to the LORD, his offering shall be of fine flour. He shall pour oil on it and put frankincense on it and bring it to Aaron's sons the priests. And he shall take from it a handful of the fine flour and oil, with all of its frankincense, and the priest shall burn this as its memorial portion on the altar, a food offering with a pleasing aroma to the LORD (Lev. 2:1-2).

> You shall present with the bread seven lambs a year old without blemish, and one bull from the herd and two rams. They shall be a burnt offering to the LORD, with their grain offering and their drink offerings, a food offering with a pleasing aroma to the LORD (Lev. 23:18).

What about the new covenant? We know that believers have to be:

> ...imitators of God, as beloved children. And walk in love, as Christ loved us and gave himself up for us, a fragrant offering and sacrifice to God (Eph. 5:1-2).

Acts of mutual love between believers come into it:

> I am well supplied, having received from Epaphroditus the gifts you sent, a fragrant offering, a sacrifice acceptable and pleasing to God (Phil. 4:18).

And the old-covenant principle can be clearly seen in:

Objections

...because of the grace given me by God to be a minister of Christ Jesus to the Gentiles in the priestly service of the gospel of God, so that the offering of the Gentiles may be acceptable, sanctified by the Holy Spirit (Rom. 15:15-16).

This, I think, is the background to, and the meaning of, Paul's use of the illustration. This is what he thanks God for:

But thanks be to God, who always leads us triumphantly as captives in Christ and through us spreads everywhere the fragrance of the knowledge of him.

Why did Paul use such illustrations? What was he saying? And why? Never forget the context! As I have explained, he was opening his extended case against the *pseudadelphoi*. He felt obliged to compare himself and his ministry with that of the *pseudadelphoi* – the super-apostles, as they were known (2 Cor. 11:5; 12:11) – with their bragging, dictatorial ways. That is why he pictured himself among the conquered slaves. The inference is unmissable: the super-apostles pictured themselves as, and acted as though they were, standing in the conqueror's chariot; Paul, however, was trudging along with the conquered.

In short, 2 Corinthians 2:14 enforces the notion of weakness, even (in human terms) of tragedy or failure. There is triumph, but that triumph belongs solely to God. Believers are conquerors – indeed, they 'are more than conquerors through him who loved' them (Rom. 8:37), and 'thanks be to God, who gives us [them] victory through our Lord Jesus Christ' (1 Cor. 15:57), but the conqueror is Christ. Moreover, look at the context of Romans 8 and 1 Corinthians 15 and you cannot miss the catalogue of suffering, weakness, loss, pain and death; the victory celebration is yet to be – at the return of Christ. And not until then!

* * *

What a pessimistic book this is, to be sure! Well... yes and no. All is not gloom and despair. Far from it. We know the narrative must end in TRIUMPH. It will!

Objections

And that takes us to the next section and chapter.

TRIUMPH

Triumph

Let me repeat the final paragraph of the previous chapter.

What a pessimistic book this is, to be sure! Well... yes and no. All is not gloom and despair. Far from it. We know the narrative must end in TRIUMPH. It will. Glorious triumph!

For a start, significant straws have been in the wind. Have you missed them?

Take Israel. As we have seen, throughout the days of the old covenant, right from Sinai, Israel played fast and loose with their covenant, kicking over the traces with regard to the law. Spiritually speaking, Israel showed her propensity to be a serial adulteress. So much so, both kingdoms eventually went into captivity under the wrath of God. There were a few bright spots – in Judah – but the reality is that the history of Israel reveals a dreadful catalogue of unfaithfulness and disobedience, one which culminated in the Jews' by-and-large rejection of the Messiah when he appeared among them, even though they had long expected him, and were (supposedly) looking forward to his coming.

And yet all this – all of it – was foreknown – indeed, prophesied – by God. He did not condone it – far from it – but none of it caught him unawares (if I might use such a phrase about the omniscient and omnipotent God).

Of all the many passages I could choose to justify my claim, let me take just one.[1]

Consider the prophet Hosea. In order to bring Israel's adultery home to the prophet, he called Hosea to live out – in his own life and experience of suffering under his tumultuous marriage to Gomer – the terrible pain of the breakdown of trust which God had had to endure from his old-covenant people:

---

[1] For more, see my *Christ*.

Triumph

Go, take to yourself a wife of whoredom and have children of whoredom, for the land [that is, Israel] commits great whoredom by forsaking the LORD (Hos. 1:2).

Worse, in naming the three offspring of the marriage, God pronounced a devastating judgment upon Israel for their unfaithfulness:

> Call [the first child's] name 'Jezreel', for in just a little while I will punish the house of Jehu for the blood of Jezreel, and I will put an end to the kingdom of the house of Israel. And on that day I will break the bow of Israel in the Valley of Jezreel...
> Call [the second child's] name 'No Mercy', for I will no more have mercy on the house of Israel, to forgive them at all...
> Call [the third child's] name 'Not My People', for you are not my people, and I am not your God (Hos. 1:4-9).

Devastating is it not? Tragic! It was a tragedy of the first water.

But in his wrath, God would remember mercy (Hab. 3:2), as he announced through Hosea:

> Yet the number of the children of Israel shall be like the sand of the sea, which cannot be measured or numbered. And in the place where it was said to them: 'You are not my people', it shall be said to them: 'Children of the living God'. And the children of Judah and the children of Israel shall be gathered together, and they shall appoint for themselves one head. And they shall go up from the land, for great shall be the day of Jezreel.
> Say to your brothers: 'You are my people', and to your sisters: 'You have received mercy'...
> Therefore, behold, I will allure her, and bring her into the wilderness, and speak tenderly to her. And there I will give her vineyards and make the Valley of Achor a door of hope. And there she shall answer as in the days of her youth, as at the time when she came out of the land of Egypt.
> And in that day, declares the LORD, you will call me 'My Husband', and no longer will you call me 'My Baal'. For I will remove the names of the Baals from her mouth, and they shall be remembered by name no more. And I will make for them a covenant on that day with the beasts of the field, the birds of the heavens, and the creeping things of the ground.

Triumph

And I will abolish the bow, the sword, and war from the land, and I will make you lie down in safety. And I will betroth you to me forever. I will betroth you to me in righteousness and in justice, in steadfast love and in mercy. I will betroth you to me in faithfulness. And you shall know the LORD.
And in that day I will answer, declares the LORD, I will answer the heavens, and they shall answer the earth, and the earth shall answer the grain, the wine, and the oil, and they shall answer 'Jezreel', and I will show her for myself in the land. And I will have mercy on 'No Mercy', and I will say to 'Not My People': 'You are my people'; and he shall say: 'You are my God'...
The children of Israel shall return and seek the LORD their God, and David their king, and they shall come in fear to the LORD and to his goodness in the latter days (Hos. 1:10 – 3:5).

And that is the merest sample of such prophecies, as I will show. To what do these prophecies refer? The restoration of Israel – that is, Judah – after exile? A miraculous conversion of most (if not all) the Jews leading to a world-wide awakening among Gentiles (postmillennialism) towards the end of this present age? A millennial, Jewish kingdom after Christ's return, lasting a 1000 years, with Christ as king reigning in Jerusalem, but ending in disaster?[2] Or what?

Certainly, the restoration of Judah after exile must come into the picture. Of that, there is no question. The prophets were, first and foremost, preaching to their own generation of pre-exile Jews. But that return cannot possibly exhaust the sweeping nature of the prophecies.[3] Some believers expect a revived Israel with a Jewish kingdom, with Christ as king,

---

[2] It is only fair to point out that some postmillennialists see a disastrous time after the glorious kingdom, and all before Christ's return. Dennis M.Swanson: 'Even postmillenarian Charles Hodge taught a rebellion at the end of the thousand years to be quelled by the personal return of Christ!' (Dennis M.Swanson: 'The Millennial Position of Spurgeon').

[3] Nor does it explain similar prophecies issue by post-exile prophets – Zech. 14:16-21; Mal. 3:1-4, for instance.

centred on Jerusalem, lasting for 1000 years – the millennium.[4] I don't share this opinion. In saying that, let me immediately add that in rejecting this 1000 year view – and, incidentally, rejecting postmillennialism (with its massive, world-wide conversion of Jews leading to a super-church kingdom before Christ returns) – I am not saying that those who hold such views are insincere, or that they do not treat the Bible seriously, and so on.[5] What is more, if I am mistaken, if either of these systems does prove correct (and one of them, at least, must be wrong), I will rejoice as much as any millennialist in the conversion of Jews in whatever form the earthly kingdom might take. But that is not how I view the prophecies.

I know those who hold one of the millennial views can quote:

...the gifts and the calling of God are irrevocable (Rom. 11:29).

But so can I. Indeed, and so do I! With the apostolic statement I wholeheartedly concur, but if it is taken to mean that God's purposes and promises concerning an everlasting covenant with Israel are certain to be fulfilled in an earthly, 1000 year kingdom, or if Romans 9 – 11 is taken to mean a world-wide revival through the conversion of the majority – if not all – the

---

[4] Based on a literal interpretation of 'Then I saw an angel coming down from heaven, holding in his hand the key to the bottomless pit and a great chain. And he seized the dragon, that ancient serpent, who is the devil and Satan, and bound him for a thousand years' (Rev. 20:1-2).

[5] But those who write on prophetical matters do not always deal fairly with opponents whose views they want to destroy, or with 'big-names' they want to corral for their view. For exposure of the way Iain Murray and Peter Masters tried to garner C.H.Spurgeon as a postmillennialist or an amillennialist respectively, see Swanson who drew heavily on C.W.H.Griffiths' 'Spurgeon's Eschatology'. The fact is, although Spurgeon was (in the main, fundamentally, broadly speaking) a fairly-standard premillennialist (my vagueness is deliberate), to consult him on prophecy is about as sensible as calling in a chameleon to advise on a colour scheme for a new kitchen.

Jews, then I disagree.[6] Not only do I find insuperable problems with both views, I also see a far greater fulfilment than either. And that fulfilment will soundly demonstrate that God's promises are beyond recall.

Take what I might call the literal interpretation leading to a 1000-year Jewish kingdom. I will be brief. This view does not seem to me to take sufficient account of the undoubted truth that God always intended the old covenant with Israel (including, of course, the shadows of the Mosaic covenant – temple, priesthood, sacrifices, sabbath, land, and so on) to be temporary (Gal. 3:23-26),[7] that the old covenant was fulfilled and rendered obsolete in the person and work of Christ (Heb 8:13):

> Let no one pass judgment on you [that is, impose on you – see Colossians 2:8] in questions of food and drink, or with regard to a festival or a new moon or a sabbath. These are a shadow of the things to come, but the substance belongs to Christ (Col. 2:16-17)...

...and that 'all the promises of God find their "Yes" in him' (2 Cor. 1:20). As Paul put it:

> Christ became a servant to the circumcised [that is, to the Jews] to show God's truthfulness, in order to confirm the promises given to the patriarchs, and in order that the Gentiles might glorify God for his mercy (Rom. 15:8-9).

In Romans 15, Paul was speaking of the gospel. In other words, it seems to me, the relevant old-covenant promises (prophecies) are spiritually fulfilled in Christ in the new covenant, and especially, I would add, in his return in glory to set up his *everlasting* kingdom. As we have seen:

> The God of heaven will set up a kingdom that shall never be destroyed, nor shall the kingdom be left to another people. It shall break in pieces all these kingdoms and bring them to an end, and it shall stand forever (Dan. 2:44).

---

[6] As for the latter, see my *Romans 11*.
[7] See my *Three*.

And, as I will argue,[8] this will occur at Christ's return in the bringing in of the everlasting kingdom.

I mention the old-covenant shadows because the prophecies in question do not hold back on predicting a glorious future-prosperity involving these shadows. Consider this:

> Then everyone who survives of all the nations that have come against Jerusalem shall go up year after year to worship the King, the LORD of hosts, and to keep the feast of booths. And if any of the families of the earth do not go up to Jerusalem to worship the King, the LORD of hosts, there will be no rain on them. And if the family of Egypt does not go up and present themselves, then on them there shall be no rain; there shall be the plague with which the LORD afflicts the nations that do not go up to keep the feast of booths. This shall be the punishment to Egypt and the punishment to all the nations that do not go up to keep the feast of booths.
> And on that day there shall be inscribed on the bells of the horses: 'Holy to the LORD'. And the pots in the house of the LORD shall be as the bowls before the altar. And every pot in Jerusalem and Judah shall be holy to the LORD of hosts, so that all who sacrifice may come and take of them and boil the meat of the sacrifice in them. And there shall no longer be a trader in the house of the LORD of hosts on that day (Zech. 14:16-21).

> [The messenger of the covenant] will sit as a refiner and purifier of silver, and he will purify the sons of Levi and refine them like gold and silver, and they will bring offerings in righteousness to the LORD. Then the offering of Judah and Jerusalem will be pleasing to the LORD as in the days of old and as in former years (Mal. 3:3-4).

And that is the merest sample.

We have to decide: were the prophets predicting that the temple, the sacrifices, the priesthood, the feasts, and all the rest, would be reinstated with renewed vigour? Or should we view their prophecies – though, naturally, issued in old-covenant

---

[8] See Appendix 1.

Triumph

language – as speaking of the new covenant? Peter, it seems to me, has given us the answer:

> Concerning this salvation [that is, the salvation accomplished through Christ in the new covenant; see the context – DG], the prophets who prophesied about the grace that was to be yours searched and inquired carefully, inquiring what person or time the Spirit of Christ in them was indicating when he predicted the sufferings of Christ and the subsequent glories. It was revealed to them that they were serving not themselves but you, in the things that have now been announced to you through those who preached the good news to you by the Holy Spirit sent from heaven, things into which angels long to look (1 Pet. 1:10-12).

Paul set out the overarching principle that governs everything in this matter:

> It is not the spiritual that is first but the natural, and then the spiritual (1 Cor. 15:46).

So it is here: there was a natural Israel with its covenant – the old covenant – and its earthly kingdom, and that came first, before the second, new, covenant for the spiritual Israel. But just as the second covenant, the superior covenant, the better covenant, the more excellent covenant, the new covenant,[9] superseded the old covenant, so Christ superseded Moses and David, and the spiritual Israel superseded the old, natural Israel. Through Christ, in Christ, the new-covenant priesthood, sacrifice, sabbath, temple, altar, whatever, superseded the old-covenant shadows. And in it all, God was fulfilling, is fulfilling and will fulfil his eternal purpose. The Jewish kingdom has vanished. The shadows have gone, never to be reinstated. What an insult it would be to Christ to reinstate any of them! What remains, what God has established, is the *ekklēsia* leading to the coming eternal kingdom of all the elect at the time of Christ's return:

> Since all these [created] things are thus to be dissolved, what sort of people ought you to be in lives of holiness and

---

[9] All these are scriptural terms (Heb. 7:19,22; 8:6; 9:15,23, and so on).

godliness, waiting for and hastening the coming of the day of God, because of which the heavens will be set on fire and dissolved, and the heavenly bodies will melt as they burn! But according to his promise we are waiting for new heavens and a new earth in which righteousness dwells (2 Pet. 3:11-13).

The creation waits with eager longing for the revealing of the sons of God. For the creation was subjected to futility, not willingly, but because of him who subjected it, in hope that the creation itself will be set free from its bondage to corruption and obtain the freedom of the glory of the children of God. For we know that the whole creation has been groaning together in the pains of childbirth until now. And not only the creation, but we ourselves, who have the firstfruits of the Spirit, groan inwardly as we wait eagerly for adoption as sons, the redemption of our bodies (Rom. 8:19-23)

Take the major prophecy of the new covenant itself (a passage just preceding, and in the context of, Jeremiah 31:35-36; see also Jer. 33:20-22):

Behold, the days are coming, declares the LORD, when I will make a new covenant with the house of Israel and the house of Judah, not like the covenant that I made with their fathers on the day when I took them by the hand to bring them out of the land of Egypt, my covenant that they broke, though I was their husband, declares the LORD. For this is the covenant that I will make with the house of Israel after those days, declares the LORD: 'I will put my law in their minds and write it on their hearts. I will be their God, and they will be my people. No longer will they teach their neighbour, or say to one another: "Know the LORD", because they will all know me, from the least of them to the greatest. For I will forgive their wickedness and will remember their sin no more' (Jer. 31:31-34).

And consider these prophecies:

It shall come to pass in the latter days that the mountain of the house of the LORD shall be established as the highest of the mountains, and shall be lifted up above the hills; and all the nations shall flow to it, and many peoples shall come, and say: 'Come, let us go up to the mountain of the LORD, to the house of the God of Jacob, that he may teach us his ways and that we may walk in his paths'. For out of Zion shall go forth

Triumph

the law, and the word of the LORD from Jerusalem (Isa. 2:2-3).

The wolf shall dwell with the lamb, and the leopard shall lie down with the young goat, and the calf and the lion and the fattened calf together; and a little child shall lead them. The cow and the bear shall graze; their young shall lie down together; and the lion shall eat straw like the ox. The nursing child shall play over the hole of the cobra, and the weaned child shall put his hand on the adder's den. They shall not hurt or destroy in all my holy mountain; for the earth shall be full of the knowledge of the LORD as the waters cover the sea (Isa. 11:6-9).

'For behold, I create new heavens and a new earth, and the former things shall not be remembered or come into mind. But be glad and rejoice forever in that which I create; for behold, I create Jerusalem to be a joy, and her people to be a gladness. I will rejoice in Jerusalem and be glad in my people; no more shall be heard in it the sound of weeping and the cry of distress. No more shall there be in it an infant who lives but a few days, or an old man who does not fill out his days, for the young man shall die a hundred years old, and the sinner a hundred years old shall be accursed. They shall build houses and inhabit them; they shall plant vineyards and eat their fruit. They shall not build and another inhabit; they shall not plant and another eat; for like the days of a tree shall the days of my people be, and my chosen shall long enjoy the work of their hands.
They shall not labour in vain or bear children for calamity, for they shall be the offspring of the blessed of the LORD, and their descendants with them. Before they call I will answer; while they are yet speaking I will hear. The wolf and the lamb shall graze together; the lion shall eat straw like the ox, and dust shall be the serpent's food. They shall not hurt or destroy in all my holy mountain', says the LORD (Isa. 65:17-25).

They [that is, Israel and Judah] shall serve the LORD their God and David their king, whom I will raise up for them (Jer. 30:9).

In those days and in that time, declares the LORD, the people of Israel and the people of Judah shall come together, weeping as they come, and they shall seek the LORD their God. They shall ask the way to Zion, with faces turned toward it, saying:

Triumph

'Come, let us join ourselves to the LORD in an everlasting covenant that will never be forgotten' (Jer. 50:4-5).

> I will set up over them one shepherd, my servant David, and he shall feed them: he shall feed them and be their shepherd. And I, the LORD, will be their God, and my servant David shall be prince among them. I am the LORD; I have spoken. I will make with them a covenant of peace... (Ezek. 34:23-25).

> Afterward the children of Israel shall return and seek the LORD their God, and David their king, and they shall come in fear to the LORD and to his goodness in the latter days (Hos. 3:5).

No doubt these prophecies have some bearing on the return of Judah from exile in Babylon. But in that return, no king was reinstated – certainly not David. I see here a prediction of Christ and his kingdom. Do not miss the references to 'the latter days'. We are talking about our present age – from Pentecost until and culminating in Christ's return.[10] And the culmination will be the new heavens and the new earth where only righteousness dwells. Triumph! God's triumph!

And, leaving aside all clues, we have the New Testament's use of the prophecies. Consider the writer of Hebrews:

> Behold, the days are coming, declares the LORD, when I will make a new covenant with the house of Israel and the house of Judah, not like the covenant that I made with their fathers on the day when I took them by the hand to bring them out of the land of Egypt, my covenant that they broke, though I was their husband, declares the LORD. For this is the covenant that I will make with the house of Israel after those days, declares the LORD: 'I will put my law in their minds and write it on their hearts. I will be their God, and they will be my people. No longer will they teach their neighbour, or say to one another: "Know the LORD", because they will all know me,

---

[10] With the ubiquitous talk of 'heaven when you die' in countless funeral sermons, hymns and sympathy cards, many believers are losing sight of the biblical hope of Christ's return, the resurrection, and eternal life in the new heavens and new *earth*. See my *Undervalued*. See my 'Waiting For Jesus' on my sermonaudio.com page, and on YouTube.

from the least of them to the greatest. For I will forgive their wickedness and will remember their sin no more' (Jer. 31:31-34; Heb. 8:7-13; 10:1-18).

Whatever is made of that quotation of the prophet, full cognisance must be taken of the writer's categorical assertion:

> In speaking of a new covenant, he [that is, God through the prophet] makes the first one obsolete. And what is becoming obsolete and growing old is ready to vanish away (Heb. 8:13).

And 'what is becoming obsolete and growing old is ready to vanish away' does not mean that the old covenant and Israel will be reinstated and active for a 1000 years after Christ's return!

Take the meeting in Jerusalem recorded in Acts 15:

> And all the assembly fell silent, and they listened to Barnabas and Paul as they related what signs and wonders God had done through them among the Gentiles. After they finished speaking, James replied: 'Brothers, listen to me. Simeon [Peter] has related how God first visited the Gentiles, to take from them a people for his name. And with this the words of the prophets agree, just as it is written...'.

James then quoted Amos:

> 'In that day I will raise up the booth of David that is fallen and repair its breaches, and raise up its ruins and rebuild it as in the days of old, that they may possess the remnant of Edom and all the nations who are called by my name', declares the LORD who does this (Amos. 9:11-12)...

...saying that God's saving of Gentiles was a fulfilment of this prophecy: 'Therefore my judgment is that we should not trouble those of the Gentiles who turn to God' (Acts 15:12-19).

Then we have Paul's use of the prophecies:

> What if God, desiring to show his wrath and to make known his power, has endured with much patience vessels of wrath prepared for destruction, in order to make known the riches of his glory for vessels of mercy, which he has prepared beforehand for glory – even us whom he has called, not from

the Jews only but also from the Gentiles? As indeed he says in Hosea: 'Those who were not my people I will call "my people", and her who was not beloved I will call "beloved". And in the very place where it was said to them: "You are not my people", there they will be called "sons of the living God"' (Rom. 9:22-26).

Paul was explicit: it is the calling of Jews and Gentiles to Christ under the gospel in the day of the new covenant that is the fulfilment of the prophecy in Hosea. Despite Israel's gross and repeated adultery, God would fulfil his eternal purpose in forming and preserving Israel; namely, the sending of his Son, the Messiah, to redeem the elect, whether Jew or Gentile, and the gathering of them through the gospel in the new covenant. Triumph! Paul applied Hosea 1:10 and 2:23 to the calling of the Gentiles (Rom. 9:24-26), yet Hosea 1:8-11 itself speaks only of the children of Israel. The context of Hosea 1 is the defection and consequent judgment of the people of Israel, and God's surprising mercy to them despite their departure from him, despite their betrayal of their covenant. The same applies to Hosea 2:23. The word 'Gentiles' does not appear in Hosea, except in Hosea 8:8, and this has no connection whatsoever with their salvation. There is no explicit reference in Hosea to the calling of the Gentiles. *But Paul set out the radically startling, new-covenant meaning of the words recorded by the prophet.*

And that is the very point I wish to make. And that is why I hope I may be forgiven for what some might consider an unnecessary and painful digression into the interpretation of prophecy. Accepting that there is a spectrum of views – premillennialism, postmillennialism, amillennialism, and seemingly endless nuances in each – I hope we can agree on the overriding point I have been trying to make: the prophecies, promises, hopes – God's eternal plan – for Israel in the old covenant have all been – or all will be – fulfilled in Christ. That is, despite Israel's miserable performance under the old covenant, nothing – nothing – could thwart the working out of God's purpose. And the same goes for the new covenant. That – and that alone – has been my purpose in my 'digression'.

Triumph

Surely, whether or not we think there will be a world-wide conversion of Jews and Gentiles, or a 1000 year Jewish kingdom,[11] it is the second coming of Christ,[12] and the establishment of the eternal kingdom that is God's ultimate purpose. As Paul put it:

> But each in his own order: Christ the firstfruits, then at his coming those who belong to Christ. Then comes the end, when [Christ] delivers the kingdom to God the Father after destroying every rule and every authority and power. For he must reign until he has put all his enemies under his feet. The last enemy to be destroyed is death... When all things are subjected to him, then the Son himself will also be subjected to him who put all things in subjection under him, that God may be all in all (1 Cor. 15:20-28).

Despite Israel's apostasy and failure, in due time – at God's appointed time – Christ did appear. He did come. And he was born an Israelite (Gal. 4:4). He did finish the work laid upon him by the Father (John 19:30). How many times Matthew recorded that such and such happened – often with Christ being totally passive – 'that it might be fulfilled which was spoken' by the prophet, or spoken by God through the prophet (Matt. 1:22; 2:15,23; 4:14; 8:17; 12:17; 13:35; 21:4; 27:35)!

And all this happened – I say it again – despite Israel's appalling record of unfaithfulness. God still accomplished his purpose in forming them into a nation; namely, the sending of his Son – the Messiah – to save sinners; that is, to save his elect (Matt. 1:21; 1 Tim. 1:15; Tit. 2:11; 3:4; Heb. 9:26). Nothing – not even Israel's apostasy – could thwart God. This is not to

---

[11] I see nothing in the post-Pentecost Scriptures to tell me this is what believers should be expecting. Rather: '[Believers] eagerly wait for the revealing of our Lord Jesus Christ' (1 Cor. 1:7). 'Our citizenship is in heaven, and from it we await a Saviour, the Lord Jesus Christ, who will transform our lowly body to be like his glorious body, by the power that enables him even to subject all things to himself' (Phil. 3:20-21).

[12] Some believers think there is more than one second coming. In their case, I am referring to the final second coming.

excuse the apostasy, but to show the sovereignty of God in action. He had determined the time, the place and the purpose of his Son's appearance (Gal. 4:4). And Christ fully accomplished all his Father's will (John 4:34; 5:30; 6:38-40; 12:28; Heb. 10:5-10); as he said:

> I always do the things that are pleasing to [the Father]... I keep his word... I have kept my Father's commandments (John 8:29,55; 15:10).

And all – all – was accomplished according to the Father's strict timetable.

Paul spelled it out:

> *At the right time* Christ died for the ungodly (Rom. 5:6).

> *When the fullness of time had come*, God sent forth his Son, born of woman, born under the law, to redeem those who were under the law, so that we might receive adoption as sons (Gal. 4:4-5).

How did Christ open his ministry? With this amazing announcement:

> *The time is fulfilled*, and the kingdom of God is at hand (Mark 1:15).

And Paul went for the big picture, speaking of:

> ...the mystery of his [that is, God's] will, according to his purpose, which he set forth in Christ as a plan *for the fullness of time*, to unite all things in him, things in heaven and things on earth (Eph. 1:9-10).

The apostle laid out the fundamental principle: 'It is not as though the word of God has failed', he declared.[13] And when he said that he was not whistling in the dark. Oh no! He had reasons – and what solid reasons they were – for his dogmatic and confident assertion. He knew how strange it would sound,

---

[13] And, as he explained, this is why Paul wrote Rom. 9 – 11. He nowhere stated that in these chapters he was setting out God's prophetical purpose of a world-wide conversion of Jews. See my *Romans 11*.

contrary to all appearance, that even with his confident assertion about God's will, he was still pressed down by the weight of the tremendous burden of wanting to see the conversion of as many of his fellow-Jews as possible; consequently, he declared: 'I am speaking the truth in Christ – I am not lying':

> I am speaking the truth in Christ – I am not lying; my conscience bears me witness in the Holy Spirit – that I have great sorrow and unceasing anguish in my heart. For I could wish that I myself were accursed and cut off from Christ for the sake of my brothers, my kinsmen according to the flesh. They are Israelites, and to them belong the adoption, the glory, the covenants, the giving of the law, the worship, and the promises. To them belong the patriarchs, and from their race, according to the flesh, is the Christ, who is God over all, blessed forever. Amen (Rom. 9:1-5).

Having made clear his longing for the conversion of his fellow-Jews (see also Romans 10:1 and remembering their privileged position under the old covenant), the apostle plunged into his argument – seeking, by his burning logic, and the warmth of his passion, to persuade as many fellow-Jews as possible to call upon Christ (Rom. 9:1 – 11:36).

What was his argument? Just this:

> But it is not as though the word of God has failed. For not all who are descended from Israel belong to Israel, and not all are children of Abraham because they are his offspring, but 'Through Isaac shall your offspring be named'. This means that it is not the children of the flesh who are the children of God, but the children of the promise are counted as offspring (Rom. 9:6-8).

And so on, and on. Piling on scriptural argument after scriptural argument, the apostle built his cast-iron case. God's eternal purpose is never thwarted. It was not thwarted – even by Israel's adultery – in the old covenant. And despite the history of the past 2000 years, God is still fulfilling his purpose in the new covenant. He is saving his elect – from among the Jews as well as Gentiles:

Triumph

> God, desiring to show his wrath and to make known his power, has endured with much patience vessels of wrath prepared for destruction, in order to make known the riches of his glory for vessels of mercy, which he has prepared beforehand for glory – even us whom he has called, not from the Jews only but also from the Gentiles... As indeed he says in Hosea: 'Those who were not my people I will call "my people", and her who was not beloved I will call "beloved". And in the very place where it was said to them: "You are not my people", there they will be called "sons of the living God"' (Rom. 9:22-26).

And that is not the end of it:

> And Isaiah cries out concerning Israel: 'Though the number of the sons of Israel be as the sand of the sea, only a remnant of them will be saved, for the LORD will carry out his sentence upon the earth fully and without delay'. And as Isaiah predicted: 'If the LORD of hosts had not left us offspring, we would have been like Sodom and become like Gomorrah' (Rom. 9:27-29).

What was the driving force behind – within – Paul? It was the logic of God's word – God's unchanging and unchangeable purpose. Listen to the apostle's eagerness pulsating in his words; feel the power, the warmth, the fire, the emotion of his all-consuming passion for the conversion of Jews. Even after 2000 years, it still flies hot off the page:

> I am speaking to you Gentiles. Inasmuch then as I am an apostle to the Gentiles, I magnify my ministry in order somehow to make my fellow-Jews jealous, and thus save some of them (Rom. 11:13-14).

And this all fitted in with what he intended to say about the amazing, staggering, will of God – how it is certain of fulfilment despite the adulterous behaviour of his professed people during both covenants:

> Lest you be wise in your own sight, I do not want you to be unaware of this mystery, brothers: a partial hardening has come upon Israel, until the fullness of the Gentiles has come

Triumph

in. And in this way all Israel [that is, all the elect in Israel – DG][14] will be saved (Rom. 11:25-26).

And, this of course, is only through Christ, his first appearance, death and resurrection:

> As it is written: 'The Deliverer will come from Zion, he will banish ungodliness from Jacob'; and 'this will be my covenant with them when I take away their sins' (Rom. 11:26-27).

Paul came to the climax:

> As regards the gospel, they [the Jews] are enemies for your [the Gentiles'] sake. But as regards election, they are beloved for the sake of their forefathers. The gifts and the calling of God are irrevocable. For just as you were at one time disobedient to God but now have received mercy because of their disobedience, so they too have now been disobedient in order that by the mercy shown to you they also may now receive mercy. For God has consigned all to disobedience, that he may have mercy on all (Rom. 11:28-32).

He concluded his argument in the only way possible:

> Oh, the depth of the riches and wisdom and knowledge of God! How unsearchable are his judgments and how inscrutable his ways! 'For who has known the mind of the LORD, or who has been his counsellor?' 'Or who has given a gift to him that he might be repaid?' For from him and through him and to him are all things. To him be glory forever. Amen (Rom. 11:33-36).[15]

Not even the devil – the arch enemy of all that is good, God's relentless foe – encouraging and using sin, even sin in God's covenant-people (Israel, and now believers), can prevent God accomplishing his purpose and sustaining his glory – without him being, in the slightest, tainted with the sin, or compromising human responsibility. And this is true, not just for Israel, not just for the *ekklēsia*, but for all the history of all mankind. And that includes Adam and his fall. What amazing

---

[14] See my *Romans 11*.
[15] For more on all this, see my *Romans 11*.

consequences have come through Christ to the world from that dreadful act![16]

As Isaac Watts put it:
> *In [Christ] the tribes of Adam boast*
> *More blessings than their father lost.*

Such is the glorious will of God! Without excusing Adam – or any of his descendants – God makes even sin to fulfil his eternal purpose. That's Triumph!

Consider Isaiah 53. After delineating the sufferings of the Messiah, the prophet came to this:

> Yet it was the will of the LORD to crush him; he has put him to grief; when his soul makes an offering for guilt, he shall see his offspring; he shall prolong his days; the will of the LORD shall prosper in his hand. Out of the anguish of his soul he shall see and be satisfied; by his knowledge shall the righteous one, my servant, make many to be accounted righteous, and he shall bear their iniquities. Therefore I will divide him a portion with the many, and he shall divide the spoil with the strong, because he poured out his soul to death and was numbered with the transgressors; yet he bore the sin of many, and makes intercession for the transgressors (Isa. 53:10-12).

Out of disaster, God brought good – and what good! Triumph!

> Thus says the LORD, he who created you, O Jacob, he who formed you, O Israel: 'Fear not, for I have redeemed you; I have called you by name, you are mine... Everyone who is called by my name, whom I created for my glory, whom I formed and made' (Isa. 43:1-7).

> O Jacob, and Israel, for you are my servant; I formed you; you are my servant; O Israel, you will not be forgotten by me... For the LORD has redeemed Jacob, and will be glorified in Israel. Thus says the LORD, your Redeemer, who formed you (Isa. 44:21-24).

> My salvation will not delay; I will put salvation in Zion, for Israel my glory (Isa. 46: 13).

---

[16] See Appendix 6.

Triumph

So much for the old covenant; now for the new:

> We [believers] are his workmanship, created in Christ Jesus for good works, which God prepared beforehand, that we should walk in them (Eph. 2:10).

Why?

> Now to him who is able to do far more abundantly than all that we ask or think, according to the power at work within us, to him be glory in the church and in Christ Jesus throughout all generations, forever and ever. Amen (Eph. 3:20-21).

> Turn to me and be saved, all the ends of the earth! For I am God, and there is no other. By myself I have sworn; from my mouth has gone out in righteousness a word that shall not return: 'To me every knee shall bow, every tongue shall swear allegiance' (Isa. 45:22-23).

> As I live, says the Lord, every knee shall bow to me, and every tongue shall confess to God (Rom. 14:11).

> Christ Jesus, who, though he was in the form of God, did not count equality with God a thing to be grasped, but emptied himself, by taking the form of a servant, being born in the likeness of men. And being found in human form, he humbled himself by becoming obedient to the point of death, even death on a cross. Therefore God has highly exalted him and bestowed on him the name that is above every name, so that at the name of Jesus every knee should bow, in heaven and on earth and under the earth, and every tongue confess that Jesus Christ is Lord, to the glory of God the Father (Phil. 2:5-11).

And this, I stress, is the very heart of the new covenant. Despite the calamitous rise of Christendom and the immense damage it has caused – and continues to cause – during 'these latter days', God is still gathering his elect. Nothing – nothing – can thwart God's purpose in Christ. As he himself declared:

> I have other sheep that are not of this fold. I must bring them also, and they will listen to my voice (John 10:16; see also John 11:52).

The elect (both Jew and Gentile; here, particularly the latter) must be saved; they will be saved; that is, they will hear, and hear effectively, Christ's call in the gospel, they will listen to it, they will be persuaded, they will turn from their sin, they will come to Christ, they will be brought to trust him, listen to all he has to say, and act upon it in obedience.

Of course, even the elect – who, by nature, as all men, are dead in sin (Eph. 2:13) – cannot believe unless, by God the Father's grace and power, the Spirit regenerates them (John 1:11-13; 3:3-8):

> You refuse to come to me that you may have life (John 5:40).

> No one can come to me unless the Father who sent me draws him. And I will raise him up on the last day. It is written in the prophets: 'And they will all be taught by God'. Everyone who has heard and learned from the Father comes to me (John 6:44-45).

And Christ was explicit in his assurance:

> All that the Father gives me will come to me, and whoever comes to me I will never cast out (John 6:37).

How well all this is illustrated by God's clarion demand that Pharaoh had to release the Israelites:

> Thus says the LORD, the God of Israel: 'Let my people go' (Ex. 5:1)...

...and by Christ's authoritative command at the grave of Lazarus:

> [Jesus] cried out with a loud voice: 'Lazarus, come out'. The man who had died came out, his hands and feet bound with linen strips, and his face wrapped with a cloth. Jesus said to them: 'Unbind him, and let him go' (John 11:43-44).

As Paul later explained:

> We know, brothers loved by God, that he has chosen you, because our gospel came to you not only in word, but also in power and in the Holy Spirit and with full conviction. You know what kind of men we proved to be among you for your sake. And you became imitators of us and of the Lord, for you received the word in much affliction, with the joy of the Holy

Triumph

Spirit, so that you became an example to all the believers in Macedonia and in Achaia. For not only has the word of the Lord sounded forth from you in Macedonia and Achaia, but your faith in God has gone forth everywhere, so that we need not say anything. For they themselves report concerning us the kind of reception we had among you, and how you turned to God from idols to serve the living and true God, and to wait for his Son from heaven, whom he raised from the dead, Jesus who delivers us from the wrath to come (1 Thess. 1:4-10).

And, as he said to the Ephesian believers:

Therefore remember that at one time you Gentiles in the flesh, called 'the uncircumcision' by what is called the circumcision, which is made in the flesh by hands – remember that you were at that time separated from Christ, alienated from the commonwealth of Israel and strangers to the covenants of promise, having no hope and without God in the world. But now in Christ Jesus you who once were far off have been brought near by the blood of Christ. For he himself is our peace, who has made us both [elect Jews and elect Gentiles] one and has broken down in his flesh the dividing wall of hostility by abolishing the law of commandments expressed in ordinances, that he might create in himself one new man in place of the two, so making peace, and might reconcile us both to God in one body through the cross, thereby killing the hostility. And he came and preached peace to you who were far off and peace to those who were near. For through him we both have access in one Spirit to the Father. So then you are no longer strangers and aliens, but you are fellow-citizens with the saints and members of the household of God, built on the foundation of the apostles and prophets, Christ Jesus himself being the cornerstone, in whom the whole structure, being joined together, grows into a holy temple in the Lord. In him you also are being built together into a dwelling place for God by the Spirit (Eph. 2:11-22).

When Paul addressed the Galatians about their conversion, he put it this way:

Now that you have come to know God, or rather to be known by God (Gal. 4:9).

John brought out the full meaning:

...this is love, not that we have loved God but that he loved us and sent his Son to be the propitiation for our sins... We love [in general; him – God – in particular] because he first loved us (1 John 4:10,19).

In short, as Christ said:

> I will build my church, and the gates of hell shall not prevail against it (Matt. 16:18).

As I said in the previous chapter, I see in Matthew 16:18 Christ's categorical assurance that the devil and all the hosts of hell will not be able to withstand God's saving call in the gospel. The elect will hear, they will heed the word, and the elect will be saved.

That's Triumph!

Not only that. God is still gathering his elect by the power of Christ through the Spirit in the gospel, yes, but that is not the whole story: this age will culminate in Christ's return in glory. Paul can assert that we – he and all believers:

> ...[are] waiting for our blessed hope, the appearing of the glory of our great God and Saviour Jesus Christ (Tit. 2:13).

> For the trumpet will sound, and the dead will be raised imperishable, and we shall be changed. For this perishable body must put on the imperishable, and this mortal body must put on immortality. When the perishable puts on the imperishable, and the mortal puts on immortality, then shall come to pass the saying that is written: 'Death is swallowed up in victory'. 'O death, where is your victory? O death, where is your sting?' The sting of death is sin, and the power of sin is the law. But thanks be to God, who gives us the victory through our Lord Jesus Christ. Therefore, my beloved brothers, be steadfast, immovable, always abounding in the work of the Lord, knowing that in the Lord your labour is not in vain (1 Cor. 15:52-58).

> Since we believe that Jesus died and rose again, even so, through Jesus, God will bring with him those who have fallen asleep. For this we declare to you by a word from the Lord, that we who are alive, who are left until the coming of the Lord, will not precede those who have fallen asleep. For the

Triumph

> Lord himself will descend from heaven with a cry of command, with the voice of an archangel, and with the sound of the trumpet of God. And the dead in Christ will rise first. Then we who are alive, who are left, will be caught up together with them in the clouds to meet the Lord in the air, and so we will always be with the Lord. Therefore encourage one another with these words (1 Thess. 4:14-18).
>
> ...when the Lord Jesus is revealed from heaven with his mighty angels in flaming fire, inflicting vengeance on those who do not know God and on those who do not obey the gospel of our Lord Jesus. They will suffer the punishment of eternal destruction, away from the presence of the Lord and from the glory of his might, when he comes on that day to be glorified in his saints, and to be marvelled at among all who have believed, because our testimony to you was believed. To this end we always pray for you, that our God may make you worthy of his calling and may fulfil every resolve for good and every work of faith by his power, so that the name of our Lord Jesus may be glorified in you, and you in him, according to the grace of our God and the Lord Jesus Christ (2 Thess. 1:7-12).

And then:

> Then I heard what seemed to be the voice of a great multitude, like the roar of many waters and like the sound of mighty peals of thunder, crying out: 'Hallelujah! For the Lord our God the Almighty reigns. Let us rejoice and exult and give him the glory, for the marriage of the Lamb has come, and his bride has made herself ready; it was granted her to clothe herself with fine linen, bright and pure' – for the fine line is the righteous deeds of the saints. And the angel said to me: 'Write this: Blessed are those who are invited to the marriage supper of the Lamb'. And he said to me: 'These are the true words of God'...
>
> Then I saw heaven opened, and behold, a white horse! The one sitting on it is called Faithful and True, and in righteousness he judges and makes war. His eyes are like a flame of fire, and on his head are many diadems, and he has a name written that no one knows but himself. He is clothed in a robe dipped in blood, and the name by which he is called is The Word of God. And the armies of heaven, arrayed in fine linen, white and pure, were following him on white horses. From his mouth comes a sharp sword with which to strike

Triumph

down the nations, and he will rule them with a rod of iron. He will tread the winepress of the fury of the wrath of God the Almighty. On his robe and on his thigh he has a name written, King of kings and Lord of lords. Then I saw an angel standing in the sun, and with a loud voice he called to all the birds that fly directly overhead: 'Come, gather for the great supper of God, to eat the flesh of kings, the flesh of captains, the flesh of mighty men, the flesh of horses and their riders, and the flesh of all men, both free and slave, both small and great'. And I saw the beast and the kings of the earth with their armies gathered to make war against him who was sitting on the horse and against his army. And the beast was captured, and with it the false prophet who in its presence had done the signs by which he deceived those who had received the mark of the beast and those who worshipped its image. These two were thrown alive into the lake of fire that burns with sulphur. And the rest were slain by the sword that came from the mouth of him who was sitting on the horse, and all the birds were gorged with their flesh (Rev. 19:6-21).

Then I saw a great white throne and him who was seated on it. From his presence earth and sky fled away, and no place was found for them. And I saw the dead, great and small, standing before the throne, and books were opened. Then another book was opened, which is the book of life. And the dead were judged by what was written in the books, according to what they had done. And the sea gave up the dead who were in it, Death and Hades gave up the dead who were in them, and they were judged, each one of them, according to what they had done. Then Death and Hades were thrown into the lake of fire. This is the second death, the lake of fire. And if anyone's name was not found written in the book of life, he was thrown into the lake of fire (Rev. 20:11-15).

And if that is not Triumph, what is?

In other words, despite all Israel's sin and failure, God still worked out his ultimate purpose in the old covenant, and – despite the *ekklēsia* becoming so enmeshed in Christendom – he will do the same in the new: in both covenants, God shows his triumphant power in and through Christ by his Spirit. This, I repeat, does not excuse Israel's sin in the days of the old covenant; nor does it excuse the *ekklēsia's* apostasy in the

Triumph

new.[17] But it does mean, as Paul put it: 'It is not as though the word of God has failed'. And that was a deliberate *litotes* – understatement – if ever there was one.

And that is why my book, though it describes dreadful apostasy, still sounds the triumphant note. Indeed, it virtually ends on that note of Triumph.[18]

Here it is:

> For the grace of God has appeared, bringing salvation for all people, training us to renounce ungodliness and worldly passions, and to live self-controlled, upright, and godly lives in the present age, waiting for our blessed hope, the appearing of the glory of our great God and Saviour Jesus Christ, who gave himself for us to redeem us from all lawlessness and to purify for himself a people for his own possession who are zealous for good works (Tit. 2:11-14).

And:

> Our [speaking of believers] citizenship is in heaven, and from it we await [that is, eagerly await, look for] a Saviour, the Lord Jesus Christ, who will transform our lowly body to be like his glorious body, by the power that enables him even to subject all things to himself (Phil. 3:20-21).

John's closing words to the last book of the Bible could not be more apposite.

The assurance:

> Behold, I am coming soon, bringing my recompense with me, to repay each one for what he has done. I am the Alpha and the Omega, the first and the last, the beginning and the end... Surely I am coming soon (Rev. 22:12-13,20).

The response:

> Amen. Come, Lord Jesus! The grace of the Lord Jesus be with all the saints. Amen (Rev. 22:20-21).[19]

---

[17] See Rev. 2 & 3.

[18] I say 'virtually' because, although 'Triumph' is the zenith, I want to bring my book to a conclusion by the chapter 'Responsibilities'.

* * *

One thing remains to be considered: in light of scriptural teaching on 'these last days' – the present calamity of the apostasy of the *ekklēsia*, and God's final triumph – what should we do?

---

[19] See my 'Waiting For Jesus' on my sermonaudio.com page, and on YouTube.

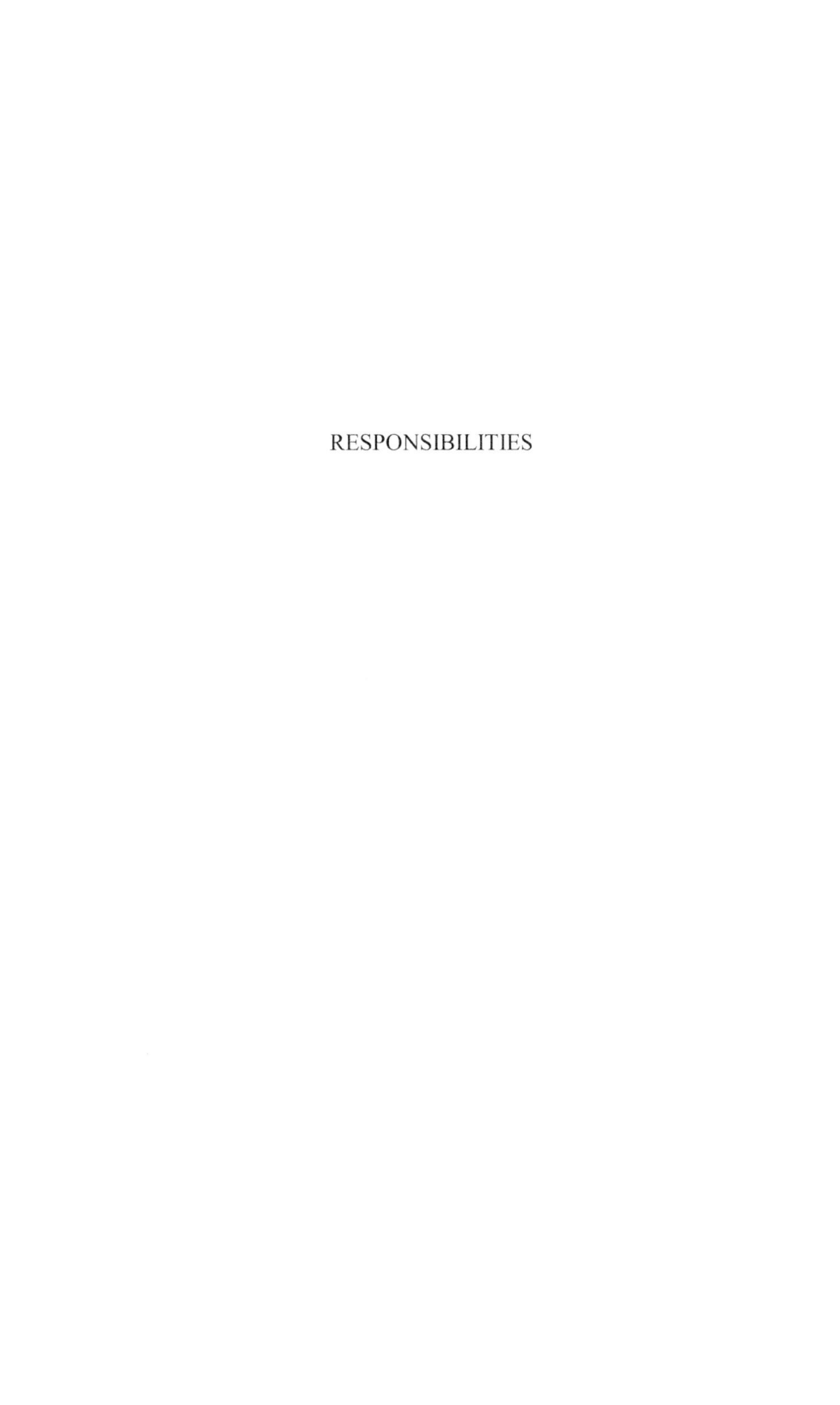

RESPONSIBILITIES

Responsibilities

I give notice that in this closing chapter I am going to ignore what is generally regarded as 'the proper thing': I am going to write, not as the pundits of political correctness demand – in the third person – but in the first and second. Getting down to brass tacks, I am going to use 'we' and 'us' and 'you' – above all, 'I' and 'me' – and not confine myself to 'them' and 'they'; I am not going to limit what I say to 'believers' in general, but talk about 'us'; in particular, I intend to speak directly to 'you', the reader. In other words, I am going to assume that my readers are fellow-believers, and write accordingly, addressing 'us' and 'you'; specifically, I am going to assume that *you* are a bornagain believer. Let me say at once that if you are not, then I have but two things to say to you, both of them said by Christ himself: 'You must be born again' (John 3:7). 'Unless you are converted... you will never enter the kingdom' (Matt. 18:3).

Why am I kicking over the traces with regard to the recognised norms of publication? Because I want to drive home what I say – to myself, and to all who read what I write. I want to convince you, and thereby see action. I do not want my words to be left – as so many preachers do these days – in the easy-to-evade and general 'they'.

So, there it is. That is the basis on which I proceed. All wrong, I dare say, but that's how it's going to be. So let's get to it.

* * *

After all that's gone before, the title of this chapter is rather silly, isn't it? After all, we know that God has determined the course of the world, that he is sovereign and unchanging, and that his eternal purpose is predetermined, unalterable and can never be thwarted; we have also come to terms with the sad truth that Christendom has marred the work of God, and will go on doing so until Christ returns; and, finally, despite the damage inflicted by Christendom, we have seen that this age –

Responsibilities

the world, indeed – will end in Triumph, God's Triumph. In light of all that, what possible responsibilities can accrue to us? What clout do we carry? What can we do about the future? *Que sera, Que sera* just about sums it up, doesn't it?[1]

No it doesn't! Of course it doesn't! The premise is right – God is sovereign, but the conclusion is wrong – all wrong – men are still responsible and accountable. We are responsible. I am. You are. *Que sera, Que sera* amounts to nothing more than fatalism.[2] And fatalism and the biblical doctrine of God's sovereignty are poles apart. Though God's sovereignty and human responsibility defeat human wit to reconcile, both are revealed in Scripture.[3] And this is why believers throughout this age have countless responsibilities – very serious responsibilities, to boot. And that, of course, applies to us today. Believers today have responsibilities in these 'times of difficulty'; that is, in these 'terrible, perilous, troublesome, dangerous, grievous times, times which are hard to bear' (2 Tim. 3:1).

In addition, as we have seen, Paul used Israel's failure under their covenant to challenge believers under their covenant (1 Cor. 10:1-14). What is more, since, in making my case, I drew heavily on Israel's poor track-record during their covenant – as a sad, foreshadowing parallel of the way the Christendom-church has treated the new covenant – it is only right and fair that we should examine the way the faithful remnant in Israel responded when they found themselves living in dark times.

---

[1] At a ministerial meeting in 1787, William Carey argued that the churches had a responsibility to take the gospel to the heathen. Allegedly, he was rebuked by John Ryland Sr: 'Sit down, young man! Sit down and be still. When God wants to convert the heathen, he will do it without consulting either you or me'. It is only fair to record that Ryland's son (also John) would later deny that his father said any such thing.

[2] Hyper-Calvinism and fatalism are bed-fellows. See my *Offer*; *Sears*; *Eternal*; *Amyraut*.

[3] See my *Offer*.

Responsibilities

How did they react? What did they do? The answers to those questions will give us guidance for our trying day.

There is no shortage of evidence – challenging evidence, I warn you. Scripture faithfully records how the remnant in Israel – those who stayed loyal to the covenant – reacted when they saw the professing people of God sinning against the Mosaic covenant and, consequently, suffering judgment for their disobedience. I said 'faithfully records', and I meant it: the faithful remnant did not pretend, they did not hide their mixed motives, but they freely vented their feelings. And the Spirit, in Scripture, honestly recorded the good as well as the bad. Yes, the best of men are men at best (and the same goes for the women, also). So why then, in the following, have I largely (but not entirely) omitted remarks made by the faithful which do not read well in the day of the new covenant? Why? Not to deceive, I assure you. Not to make out that these men and women were purer than pure.[4] Certainly not! Indeed, doing that would defeat my purpose. The people I quote were sinners no less than we are, as mixed as we are. Let me speak for myself: I do not claim to have unmixed motives in writing and preaching. I say that, not to brag, but to own it. I dare say that my readers will admit their own mixed motives, even as they read and listen. The fact is, I want to stress that while the godly, during the time of the old covenant, did not always react in their dark day as they should have done, nevertheless by their stance for the truth, and by their grief over the sins of the people, they pointedly challenge us today. And that is why I write.

And that leads me to speak about things which are painful to raise; I am talking personally again. I referred to the faithful remnant in the days of the old covenant, and the rebuke their

---

[4] Those who follow Eusebius, and write hagiography rather than history, do their heroes no service. Nor does it help those who read. Giving the impression that a fellow-believer is faultless is little use to a believer who knows he (himself) or she (herself) to be anything but. Oliver Cromwell's 'warts and all' is pertinent. The Spirit never disguises. Take the record of David, as but one example. Take Peter's denial of Christ, and all the disciples' desertion, as other sad cases.

Responsibilities

behaviour presents to believers today. No one needs that rebuke more than I. Alas, I have to confess that is easy to write, argue and preach about the dire state of the *ekklēsia* during the reign of Christendom, and give the impression of being righteously indignant about it, but God's call is for me to feel – to feel – what I write about.

That's not all. I also fail – sin, compromise – under Christendom. I confess it. As before, I am not boasting about it, but admitting it. But how can I do any good to my fellow-believers unless I, to a certain extent, get involved in Christendom? That's the dilemma. It's a nut I don't know how to crack.

Nevertheless, this kind of dilemma is not unique. Let me illustrate. During the Second World War, while the Nazis did all they could to keep their industrial slaughter of millions of Jews and countless others under wraps, the news seeped out. Added to which, towards the end of the war, the Americans liberated airfields which would enable them to fly bombers to places such as Auschwitz, discharge their load, and fly back. Appeals were made to the powers-that-be that the Americans should do this very thing, and put an end to the genocide. Harrowing debates were held in high places. The leaders weighed the pros and cons. Some changed their mind. The pros included the end of the slaughter (at least at the camp that had been bombed), and, supremely, it would let the Nazi High Command know that, despite their elaborate attempts to avoid detection, their diabolical secret was out, and that those responsible would be held to account. The cons included the inaccuracy of bombing in those days, the deliberate slaughter of thousands of Jewish and other victims, the certainty that the Nazis would force the survivors to footslog their way out of reach and to their death, and the certain, virulent reaction of the vocal anti-Semite lobby in the USA at the inevitable death of American servicemen in carrying out the bombing. The decision was taken: not to bomb. But immediately many of those involved had serious doubts: Were we right not to bomb? But they knew that if the decision had gone the other way, they

Responsibilities

would have been harrowed by another question. Were we right to bomb?

While not claiming that my decision – I say 'my decision', but I know I am not alone, far from it – is in that class, it amounts to the same for me, personally. Do I compromise somewhat with Christendom so that I might do some good to those within it? Or do I cut myself off altogether? Not that is it possible to do the latter – and herein lies a major part of the problem. Whatever I do – or don't do – I am enmeshed in Christendom from the cradle to the grave. Catch-22 doesn't get near it![5]

Here is the dilemma.

Paul was adamant about the duty of believers to try to edify fellow-believers:

> Let us pursue what makes for peace and for mutual up-building (Rom. 14:19).

> ...for their up-building and encouragement and consolation... [builds] up the *ekklēsia*... so that the *ekklēsia* may be built up... Strive to excel in building up the *ekklēsia*... built up... Let all things be done for building up (1 Cor. 14:3-5,12,17,26).

It might be tempting, therefore, to try to get out of the system, stop doing anything to bolster the system, avoid the institutional altogether, and stop preaching and writing through Christendom means, and so stop compromising, But I am then immediately faced with wondering how I can obey the biblical command, meet with fellow-believers, and engage in mutual edification? And that duty is expressly stated by the writer of Hebrews:

> Exhort one another every day...
> Let us hold fast the confession of our hope without wavering, for he who promised is faithful. And let us consider how to stir up one another to love and good works, not neglecting to meet together, as is the habit of some, but encouraging one another,

---

[5] *Catch-22*, a 1961 novel by Joseph Heller, gave rise to the phrase. It has come to mean that whichever of two possibilities you choose, you will be wrong.

and all the more as you see the Day drawing near (Heb. 3:13; 10:23-25.

Nor does it solve my problem saying that in my experience there is precious little mutual edification in Christendom-churches: if I don't ever meet fellow-believers, or engage with them, how can I do them any good, or receive from them?

In any case, opting-out is impossible. I don't have the choice. As long as I live, I live in Christendom. Escapism, isolationism, living in a bubble, though it looks inviting, is not actually on the table.

However, there is a sterling example of encouragement: Paul, and his desire to preach Christ to his fellow-Jews. I will return to this – to speak of the apostle's love for sinners – but at this point I concentrate on his willingness to use the synagogue to address Jews. While he knew that Christ had fulfilled the old covenant and rendered it obsolete, that Judaism was a thing of the past, even so, it was his usual practice – if necessary – to attend the synagogue on the sabbath so that he might address Jews with the gospel (Acts 13:14,42-44; 14:1; 17:1-2,10,16-17; 18:4,19; 19:8). In Philippi, where (in all probability) there was no synagogue, the apostle sought out a gathering of Jewish women on the sabbath (Acts 16:13), sitting down with them so that he could speak to them.

Moreover, I am confronted by the way the faithful in Israel comported themselves under the nation's desertion from the Mosaic covenant. They got stuck in. Rather like certain characters we meet in the Gospels – the lad with his picnic lunch (John 6:9), the poor widow with her two mites (Mark 12:42), and the woman with her ointment (Mark 14:8) – they did what they could, when they could, where they could; they gave what they had. And, of course, as I have said, it's not just me: I want to encourage other like-minded believers to emulate all that was best in the faithful remnant under the old covenant. And what about the many believers that have never thought about the issue? Can't I say something which might provoke them, even awaken them? That is the spirit in which I write.

Responsibilities

* * *

Let me start with what, speaking for myself, is the most painful of all the painful lessons we can draw from the behaviour of the old-covenant faithful.

In times of apostasy, faithful believers must show a brokenness of spirit

We know that while the unfaithful prophets were encouraging Israel to play fast and loose with the Mosaic covenant and its law, assuring them of God's blessing in their sinful behaviour (Isa. 9:15-16; Jer. 37:19; Ezek. 13:1-7; 22:25,28, for instance), the faithful prophets were continually calling Israel and Judah back to obedience to the old covenant. And nearly always their labours – or so it seemed to them – met a brick wall; they felt themselves to be utter failures; the professing people of God grew hardened in their disobedience, closing their ears, minds and hearts to God's call. How did the prophets react? In addition to my earlier caveat about their mixed motives, I have to say that it is not always easy to unravel what the prophets said, and so determine their own personal feelings. The prophets' words had a threefold application: to the nation, supremely to the Messiah, but also to what the prophets themselves were feeling. Hence the difficulty. Even so, as for the latter, certain things stand out.

Let me start with Moses. How did he react when, having received the law, he came down from Sinai only to be confronted by the people's blatant idolatry? It goes without saying that he rebuked the people. He certainly did that! He told them:

> You have sinned a great sin (Ex. 32:30).

But, having rebuked his fellow-Jews, he did not stop at that:

> You have sinned a great sin. And now I will go up to the LORD; perhaps I can make atonement for your sin (Ex. 32:30).

Responsibilities

He re-climbed the mountain and prayed for the people! And we know the burden of his prayer when he reached the top of Sinai:

> Alas, this people has sinned a great sin. They have made for themselves gods of gold. But now, if you will forgive their sin – but if not, please blot me out of your book that you have written (Ex. 32:31-32).

What an attitude! What a challenge!

To move on: how honest is Scripture concerning Elijah! Having just been used in a great spiritual victory over Ahab and the prophets of Baal, how he must have been congratulating himself, counting the number of 'likes' on social media! Not a bit of it:

> He was afraid, and he arose and ran for his life... And he asked that he might die, saying: 'It is enough; now, O LORD, take away my life, for I am no better than my fathers' (1 Kings 19:3-4).

Now there's a reaction and a half! I am not saying that present-day believers who are grieved about the state of the *ekklēsia* should go to such extremes. No! But it is clear that Elijah was far from smug, that he had no sense of patting himself on the back and puffing out his chest. He knew nothing of the spirit of the Pharisee (Luke 18:11);[6] if I may accommodate that man's words:

> God, I thank you that I am not like these Jews, tangled in paganism.

Bringing it home to believers today, he did not say:

> God, I thank you that I am not like other men, tangled in Christendom.

Indeed, Elijah had a far-too gloomy a view of himself and what was really going on in the nation. When God probed him about why he was depressed, the prophet replied:

---

[6] Original 'God, I thank you that I am not like other men, extortioners, unjust, adulterers, or even like this tax collector'.

Responsibilities

> I have been very jealous for the LORD, the God of hosts. For the people of Israel have forsaken your covenant, thrown down your altars, and killed your prophets with the sword, and I, even I only, am left, and they seek my life, to take it away (1 Kings 19:10).

How wrong could he have been! Far too pessimistic, as God told him:

> I will leave seven thousand in Israel, all the knees that have not bowed to Baal, and every mouth that has not kissed him (1 Kings 19:18).

Paul made sure that believers – though living in the day of the new covenant – got the significance of these words for their own time:

> Do you not know what the Scripture says of Elijah, how he appeals to God against Israel? 'Lord, they have killed your prophets, they have demolished your altars, and I alone am left, and they seek my life'. But what is God's reply to him? 'I have kept for myself seven thousand men who have not bowed the knee to Baal'. So too at the present time there is a remnant, chosen by grace. But if it is by grace, it is no longer on the basis of works; otherwise grace would no longer be grace (Rom. 11:2-6).

And so, despite his former depression, Elijah pressed on, anointing Elisha, and so on (1 Kings 19:19-21). Now there's a lesson!

Take Isaiah's heartfelt complaint. As his entire prophecy makes clear, he had pulled no punches over Judah's defection.[7] Can anyone doubt that he himself was one of 'those who mourn in Zion' (Isa. 61:3)? And we know about his frustration, and why he had a dark sense of disappointment: he had preached, preached faithfully; he had prophesied, he had warned, he had pleaded, but all in vain; nothing moved the people; he had been talking to the deliberately deaf:

---

[7] See my *Evangelicals*.

Responsibilities

Who has believed what he has heard from us? And to whom has the arm of the LORD been revealed? (Isa. 53:1).[8]

That doesn't need much unpacking. The prophet was convinced of God's sovereignty, but struggled under a sense of his own failure to influence the people. And the following extract, while the nation is in view, surely gives us a glimpse into Isaiah's own desperate experience:

> Listen to me, O coastlands, and give attention, you peoples from afar. The LORD called me from the womb, from the body of my mother he named my name. He made my mouth like a sharp sword; in the shadow of his hand he hid me; he made me a polished arrow; in his quiver he hid me away. And he said to me: 'You are my servant, Israel, in whom I will be glorified'. But I said: 'I have laboured in vain; I have spent my strength for nothing and vanity; yet surely my right is with the LORD, and my recompense with my God' (Isa. 49:1-4).

Jeremiah also:

> My joy is gone; grief is upon me; my heart is sick within me. Behold, the cry of the daughter of my people from the length and breadth of the land: 'Is the LORD not in Zion? Is her King not in her?' 'Why have they provoked me to anger with their carved images and with their foreign idols?' 'The harvest is past, the summer is ended, and we are not saved'. For the wound of the daughter of my people is my heart wounded; I mourn, and dismay has taken hold on me. Is there no balm in Gilead? Is there no physician there? Why then has the health of the daughter of my people not been restored? (Jer. 8:18-22).

And the prophet's grief is palpable here:

> Hear, O women, the word of the LORD, and let your ear receive the word of his mouth; teach to your daughters a lament, and each to her neighbour a dirge. For death has come up into our windows; it has entered our palaces, cutting off the

---

[8] This passage plays into the way the Jews rejected Christ (John 12:38-43) and sinners reject the gospel (Rom. 10:16), but it also shows us how Isaiah himself felt. At this time, of course, I am concerned with what we can learn about the way believers react to the new covenant.

Responsibilities

children from the streets and the young men from the squares (Jer. 9:20-21).

Furthermore, seeing what was coming, the prophet tried yet again to call the people back to God and the covenant, warning them of the dreadful consequence of refusal:

> Hear and give ear; be not proud, for the LORD has spoken. Give glory to the LORD your God before he brings darkness, before your feet stumble on the twilight mountains, and while you look for light he turns it into gloom and makes it deep darkness. But if you will not listen, my soul will weep in secret for your pride; my eyes will weep bitterly and run down with tears, because the LORD's flock has been taken captive (Jer. 13:15-17).

God was determined to punish Judah, as he had punished Israel, and this would be unspeakably grievous for the people (Jer. 15:1-9). The nation would be virtually friendless. Jeremiah, knowing this, did all he could to awaken the people:

> Who will have pity on you, O Jerusalem, or who will grieve for you? Who will turn aside to ask about your welfare? (Jer. 15:5).

Jeremiah had done all he could to bring the people back to obedience to God. And how had they reacted to all the prophet's pleadings, warnings and encouragements? Like this:

> Woe is me, my mother, that you bore me, a man of strife and contention to the whole land! I have not lent, nor have I borrowed, yet all of them curse me (Jer. 15:10).

Jeremiah honestly recorded his reaction:

> O LORD, you know; remember me and visit me, and take vengeance for me on my persecutors. In your forbearance take me not away; know that for your sake I bear reproach. Your words were found, and I ate them, and your words became to me a joy and the delight of my heart, for I am called by your name, O LORD, God of hosts. I did not sit in the company of revellers, nor did I rejoice; I sat alone, because your hand was upon me, for you had filled me with indignation. Why is my pain unceasing, my wound incurable, refusing to be healed?

Responsibilities

Will you be to me like a deceitful brook, like waters that fail? (Jer. 15:15-18; see also, Jer. 20:1-18).

God reassured the prophet (Jer. 15:19-21; 31:16). But still the poor man felt he had to write an entire book entitled Lamentations, in the opening of which he poured out a cataract of Jerusalem's sorrows. In recording this, he did not gloat with a cheery 'I told you so!' (*cf.* Jas. 1:5), but declared:

> For these things I weep; my eyes flow with tears; for a comforter is far from me, one to revive my spirit; my children are desolate, for the enemy has prevailed (Lam. 1:16).

That extract speaks of the weeping of the city, the city personified. But I can also hear Jeremiah's own spirit in the words. He saw the trouble coming; he knew it was deserved; but still he grieved. And certainly his feelings are made plain in this:

> My eyes are spent with weeping; my stomach churns; my bile is poured out to the ground because of the destruction of the daughter of my people, because infants and babies faint in the streets of the city.
> They cry to their mothers: 'Where is bread and wine?' as they faint like a wounded man in the streets of the city, as their life is poured out on their mothers' bosom.
> What can I say for you, to what compare you, O daughter of Jerusalem? What can I liken to you, that I may comfort you, O virgin daughter of Zion? For your ruin is vast as the sea; who can heal you?
> Your prophets have seen for you false and deceptive visions; they have not exposed your iniquity to restore your fortunes, but have seen for you oracles that are false and misleading (Lam. 2:11-14).

> Look, O LORD, and see! With whom have you dealt thus? Should women eat the fruit of their womb, the children of their tender care? Should priest and prophet be killed in the sanctuary of the Lord?
> In the dust of the streets lie the young and the old; my young women and my young men have fallen by the sword; you have killed them in the day of your anger, slaughtering without pity (Lam. 2:20-21).

Responsibilities

The agony Jeremiah endured cost him: it had made him ill, both physically and emotionally (Lam. 3:1-20). Uncontrollable weeping had overtaken him:

> All our enemies open their mouths against us; panic and pitfall have come upon us, devastation and destruction; my eyes flow with rivers of tears because of the destruction of the daughter of my people.
> My eyes will flow without ceasing, without respite, until the LORD from heaven looks down and sees; my eyes cause me grief at the fate of all the daughters of my city (Lam. 3:46-51).

Now there's a challenge, if ever there was one!

And when, after Judah had been taken into captivity, and its capital utterly wasted, Nehemiah, on hearing grim news about Jerusalem – even before he had made a personal inspection of the city ruins – was heart-stricken at the thought of the dreadful state of Jerusalem (Neh. 1:1-4). It had robbed him of sleep, no doubt, and taken away his appetite for food. This is not mere speculation: King Artaxerxes could see the anguish plainly etched on Nehemiah's face, and raised the issue with his servant (Neh. 2:1-8). Whatever may be said about Nehemiah, nobody could ever accuse him of living in an ivory tower.

Even after Judah's return from exile, the Jews were intermarrying with pagans. Ezra, when he heard of this, recorded his reaction:

> As soon as I heard this, I tore my garment and my cloak and pulled hair from my head and beard and sat appalled (Ezra 9:3).

He confessed his sense of shame in prayer to God, and led the people in weeping before the LORD (Ezra 9:4 – 10:1).

That is just a sample of how the faithful reacted in dark days during the old covenant. If such examples do not challenge us, nothing will. But there is more to come.

Let us think about Christ. We know that 'he came to his own [that is, the Jews], and his own people did not receive him' (John 1:11), that he 'endured the hostility of sinners against

Responsibilities

himself' (Heb. 12:3), that he was 'reproached' (Rom. 15:3).[9] How did he react? He could have called upon 'more than twelve legions of angels' (Matt. 26:53) to deliver him, wreaking vengeance on his enemies. But he refused. Again, when the Samaritans would not welcome him, and he was confronted by James and John who want to call fire down from heaven, yet again he refused, rebuking his disciples in the process (Luke 9:51-55). The Lord Jesus showed his forgiving spirit in these remarkable words:

> O Jerusalem, Jerusalem, the city that kills the prophets and stones those who are sent to it! How often would I have gathered your children together as a hen gathers her brood under her wings, and you were not willing! See, your house is left to you desolate. For I tell you, you will not see me again, until you say: 'Blessed is he who comes in the name of the Lord' (Matt. 23:37-39).

> When he drew near and saw the city, he wept over it, saying: 'Would that you, even you, had known on this day the things that make for peace! But now they are hidden from your eyes. For the days will come upon you, when your enemies will set up a barricade around you and surround you and hem you in on every side and tear you down to the ground, you and your children within you. And they will not leave one stone upon another in you, because you did not know the time of your visitation' (Luke 19:41-44).

And we have his prayer in his dying moments:

> Daughters of Jerusalem, do not weep for me, but weep for yourselves and for your children. For behold, the days are coming when they will say: 'Blessed are the barren and the wombs that never bore and the breasts that never nursed!' Then they will begin to say to the mountains: 'Fall on us', and to the hills: 'Cover us'. For if they do these things when the wood is green, what will happen when it is dry?... Father, forgive them, for they know not what they do' (Luke 23:28-34).

---

[9] See, for instance, Matt. 11:19; 26:25; 27:39; John 8:48.

Responsibilities

It is precisely at this point that believers need to take full account of Peter's uncompromising words:

> Christ also suffered for you, leaving you an example, so that you might follow in his steps (1 Pet. 2:21).

I acknowledge that 'suffering' is Peter's point, but Christ's forgiving attitude surely cannot be excluded. Believers are called 'to follow' Christ (Matt. 11:29; 16:24), not least in having a forgiving spirit.

And so to Paul. Even though he had met many disappointments (Acts 9:16), and although he knew that believers would always have to face such (Acts 14:22; 20:29-30), as he told Timothy he had remained steadfast (2 Tim. 4:6-8). Moreover, he said this in the context of urging all other believers to do the same (2 Tim. 4:1-8). But there was no bitterness in the apostle. As he explained to the Ephesian elders when he called them together at Miletus:

> Therefore be alert, remembering that for three years I did not cease night or day to admonish every one with tears (Acts 20:31).

And he felt, and felt deeply, what he was saying:

> I am speaking the truth in Christ – I am not lying; my conscience bears me witness in the Holy Spirit – that I have great sorrow and unceasing anguish in my heart. For I could wish that I myself were accursed and cut off from Christ for the sake of my brothers, my kinsmen according to the flesh. They are Israelites, and to them belong the adoption, the glory, the covenants, the giving of the law, the worship, and the promises. To them belong the patriarchs, and from their race, according to the flesh, is the Christ, who is God over all, blessed forever. Amen (Rom. 9:1-5).

> Brothers, my heart's desire and prayer to God for them is that they may be saved. For I bear them witness that they have a zeal for God, but not according to knowledge. For, being ignorant of the righteousness of God, and seeking to establish their own, they did not submit to God's righteousness. For Christ is the end of the law for righteousness to everyone who believes (Rom. 10:1-4).

Responsibilities

For though I am free from all, I have made myself a servant to all, that I might win more of them. To the Jews I became as a Jew, in order to win Jews. To those under the law I became as one under the law (though not being myself under the law) that I might win those under the law. To those outside the law I became as one outside the law (not being outside the law of God but under the law of Christ) that I might win those outside the law. To the weak I became weak, that I might win the weak. I have become all things to all people, that by all means I might save some. I do it all for the sake of the gospel, that I may share with them in its blessings (1 Cor. 9:19-23).

Ever the preacher, the apostle made application wherever he could:

Brothers, join in imitating me, and keep your eyes on those who walk according to the example you have in us. For many, of whom I have often told you and now tell you even with tears, walk as enemies of the cross of Christ. Their end is destruction, their god is their belly, and they glory in their shame, with minds set on earthly things (Phil. 3:17-19).

'Even with tears'. Yes, he confronted apostates. Yes, he challenged rebels. But he did it with tears streaming down his cheeks. I'll say it again: if such examples do not move us, nothing will.

Believers must continue to work for God, stirred by the thought of God's sovereignty

Really? Yes, indeed! Contrary to what might be considered the logical stance, those who are most persuaded of God's sovereignty are often among the most workish. The Bible is replete with accounts of the lives of men and women who, while they were fully persuaded that God is sovereign and that he has predetermined and controls all events – and rejoice in it – nevertheless have been determined and resolute in being sacrificially active for God. Persuasion of God's sovereignty never put any damper on their efforts. Quite the reverse. God's sovereignty was not a soporific sending them to sleep, or a cushion to lie their head on; it was a stimulus. So much so, they were living proofs of the biblical maxim:

Responsibilities

The people who know their God shall stand firm and take action (Dan. 11:32).

Or, as the KJV puts it:

The people that do know their God shall be strong, and do exploits.

Notice that. Be firm, be strong. But that's not all: get on with the work!

We may take this further.

Believers must continue to work for God despite difficulty

Scripture records the lives of men and women who, although they realised the task they faced was, to put it mildly, going to be difficult, nevertheless pressed on, persevering despite many obstacles, setbacks and disappointments.

Take Abraham:

In hope he believed against hope, that he should become the father of many nations, as he had been told: 'So shall your offspring be'. He did not weaken in faith when he considered his own body, which was as good as dead (since he was about a hundred years old), or when he considered the barrenness of Sarah's womb. No unbelief made him waver concerning the promise of God, but he grew strong in his faith as he gave glory to God, fully convinced that God was able to do what he had promised (Rom. 4:18-21).

Yes, he had God's promise, but it was far from plain sailing all the way for him. He faced the acid test – and came through with colours flying – when God called him to sacrifice Isaac:

By faith Abraham, when he was tested, offered up Isaac, and he who had received the promises was in the act of offering up his only son, of whom it was said: 'Through Isaac shall your offspring be named'. He considered that God was able even to raise him from the dead, from which, figuratively speaking, he did receive him back (Heb. 11:17-19).

As Hebrews 12 goes on to say, such examples are recorded to stimulate us to labour on despite all difficulties:

Responsibilities

> Therefore, since we are surrounded by so great a cloud of witnesses, let us run with endurance the race that is set before us (Heb. 12:1).

Do not miss the 'therefore'. And do not mistake the 'let us'; it is not a good idea, a gentle suggestion; it is a command!

What is more, the writer of Hebrews immediately went on to raise the bar to the highest level:

> Therefore, since we are surrounded by so great a cloud of witnesses, let us also lay aside every weight, and sin which clings so closely, and let us run with endurance the race that is set before us, ***looking to Jesus, the founder and perfecter of our faith, who for the joy that was set before him endured the cross, despising the shame***, and is seated at the right hand of the throne of God (Heb. 12:1-2).

Take Ezra and Nehemiah, and the prophets Zechariah, Haggai and Malachi. They knew they were facing an uphill task, a mammoth task – one might say, a well-nigh impossible task. For God had called upon them, after the return of the Jews from the seventy-years' exile in Babylon, to stir the people to roll up their sleeves, get down to the back-breaking task of removing the heaps of rubble in Jerusalem – both materially and spiritually – rubble that had accumulated as a result of the people's sin over many years, and brought about by the devastation of the Babylonian invasion, and the years of neglect which had followed, and put in place positive scriptural reforms. Their aim – and what an aim it was! – to rebuild, not only Jerusalem in a physical sense, but Judaism in its entirety – not just the temple. One would have thought the temple would have been enough; it would have been more than enough for most men! But did these stalwarts gasp and gape at the enormity of the task, wring their hands, and gripe? They were grieved by what they saw, yes. As they uncovered the full extent of Judah's ruin, and the degradation that Jerusalem and Judaism had suffered, they were deeply distressed. As we have already seen, Nehemiah, even before he had made a personal inspection of the disaster area, was heart-stricken on hearing of the dreadful state of Jerusalem (Neh. 1:1-4). So much so, King

Responsibilities

Artaxerxes could see the anguish plainly etched on Nehemiah's face, and raised the issue with his servant (Neh. 2:1-8). Oh, yes, he was grieved, but not reduced to inaction.

Moreover, as we have already noted, the devastation went much further and cut much deeper than stones and timber; the people – even after return from exile – were intermarrying with pagans. Ezra, when he heard of this return to apostasy recorded his reaction:

> As soon as I heard this, I tore my garment and my cloak and pulled hair from my head and beard and sat appalled (Ezra 9:3).

He confessed his sense of shame in prayer to God, and led the people in weeping before the LORD (Ezra 9:4 – 10:1).

But these two men did not stop at grief; they went further, much further. Did they pray? Of course they did (Neh. 1:4-11; 2:4; 4:9, and so on). But, above all, when they were given the chance to begin the work of reform – both negative and positive – these men grabbed it with both hands.

Despite the harrowing pain involved for all concerned, Ezra immediately set about reversing the marriages with pagans (Ezra 10:2-44).

And, when he reached the city, Nehemiah lost no time in making a through, personal inspection of the ruins (Neh. 2:11-15).

He was mortified – but not petrified.[10] He called the people together, and was blunt with them:

> 'You see the trouble we are in, how Jerusalem lies in ruins with its gates burned. Come, let us build the wall of Jerusalem, that we may no longer suffer derision'. And I told them of the hand of my God that had been upon me for good, and also of the words that the king had spoken to me. And they said: 'Let

---

[10] Literally, 'turned to stone'; so badly affected that he could do nothing.

Responsibilities

us rise up and build'. So they strengthened their hands for the good work (Neh. 2:17-18).

No doubt Nehemiah, along with Ezra and the three prophets, Zechariah, Haggai and Malachi, recalled God's opening words to Jeremiah when he had been commissioned to God's work, spoken by the LORD more than seventy years before, words spoken in light of the appalling judgment God was about to unleash on his people because of their betrayal of the covenant:

> I have set you this day over nations and over kingdoms, to pluck up and to break down, to destroy and to overthrow, to build and to plant (Jer. 1:10).

Moreover, Jeremiah had known that he was going to suffer for his preaching:

> I am calling all the tribes of the kingdoms of the north, declares the LORD, and they shall come, and every one shall set his throne at the entrance of the gates of Jerusalem, against all its walls all around and against all the cities of Judah. And I will declare my judgments against them, for all their evil in forsaking me. They have made offerings to other gods and worshipped the works of their own hands. But you, dress yourself for work; arise, and say to them everything that I command you. Do not be dismayed by them, lest I dismay you before them. And I, behold, I make you this day a fortified city, an iron pillar, and bronze walls, against the whole land, against the kings of Judah, its officials, its priests, and the people of the land. They will fight against you, but they shall not prevail against you, for I am with you, declares the LORD, to deliver you (Jer. 1:15-19).

Hosea, likewise had known what Israel thought about him and others like him:

> The prophet is a fool; the man of the spirit is mad [is a maniac], because of your [that is, Israel's] great iniquity and great hatred (Hos. 9:7).[11]

---

[11] Christ met the same (Mark 3:21; John 10:20), as did Paul (Acts 26:24).

Responsibilities

The subsequent history of Judah recorded in the *post*-exile books never glosses over the personal abuse men such as Ezra and Nehemiah had to endure from their fellow-Jews, the enemies (with their diabolical schemes) they had to counter, the disappointments they had to swallow, the inward and outward cost they had to meet, the terrifying decisions they had to take, and the excruciating personal reforms they had to impose on the people. But – nothing daunted – they threw themselves into the work, and, moreover, they saw it through. As Nehemiah could justly say: 'Remember me, O my God, concerning this, and do not wipe out my good deeds that I have done for the house of my God and for his service' (Neh. 13:14; see also Neh. 5:19; 13:22,31).

The three aforesaid prophets, likewise, despite repeated backsliding by the people, went on preaching with vehemence and passion – rebuking, encouraging, stirring the people to turn from their carnality and get the work done. I am reminded of Paul's encouragement to Archippus:

> See that you fulfil the ministry that you have received in the Lord (Col. 4:17).

And the work was done! They did 'fulfil their ministry'. Although the rebuilt temple fell far short of the glory days of Solomon's early years (Ezra 3:12-13), all the above-mentioned men devoted their lives to do what they could, as Zechariah put it, in 'the day of small things' (Zech. 4:10). They threw themselves – heart and soul – into the work of reform, and called others to do the same – even in a day of ruin.

The lesson is clear: if we really are living in the day of apostasy, then we must do what we can, even though it is in a day of small things, a day dark and difficult, a day which presents questions beyond solution.

The point can be taken even further.

Responsibilities

Believers must continue to work for God despite knowing that failure is certain

Scripture tells us of people who faced an even more daunting prospect than knowing that the task before them was going to be difficult; they knew that disaster was coming; they knew that their labour was doomed to failure.[12] God had told them so. Nevertheless, remarkably,[13] they still did all they could for God. This, no doubt, sounds utterly illogical. It is! But human logic, human reason, is never to be the believer's guide. Scripture by the Spirit is.

Take Josiah, one-time king of Judah. We know that his grandfather, Manasseh, had sinned so grievously that the LORD had issued a dreadful judgment:

> Because Manasseh king of Judah has committed these abominations [recorded in 2 Kings 21] and has done things more evil than all that the Amorites did, who were before him, and has made Judah also to sin with his idols, therefore thus says the LORD, the God of Israel: Behold, I am bringing upon Jerusalem and Judah such disaster that the ears of everyone who hears of it will tingle. And I will stretch over Jerusalem the measuring line of Samaria, and the plumb line of the house of Ahab, and I will wipe Jerusalem as one wipes a dish, wiping it and turning it upside down. And I will forsake the remnant of my heritage and give them into the hand of their

---

[12] In the days of the new covenant, believers, though they might strongly suspect it, cannot *know* that failure is certain. But take a similar example from the days of the old covenant – Jonah. He eventually went to Nineveh even though he strongly suspected that God would spare the Ninevites when they repented upon being told of their doom: 'O LORD, is not this what I said when I was yet in my country? That is why I made haste to flee to Tarshish; for I knew that you are a gracious God and merciful, slow to anger and abounding in steadfast love, and relenting from disaster. Therefore now, O LORD, please take my life from me, for it is better for me to die than to live' (Jonah 4:2-3). Did Jonah want the Ninevites judged? Was he angry because God had thwarted him?

[13] 'Remarkably' or 'surprisingly', is too weak; it should be thought of as something which is staggering or astonishing.

Responsibilities

enemies, and they shall become a prey and a spoil to all their enemies, because they have done what is evil in my sight and have provoked me to anger, since the day their fathers came out of Egypt, even to this day (2 Kings 21:10-15).

> I will appoint over them four kinds of destroyers, declares the LORD: the sword to kill, the dogs to tear, and the birds of the air and the beasts of the earth to devour and destroy. And I will make them a horror to all the kingdoms of the earth because of what Manasseh the son of Hezekiah, king of Judah, did in Jerusalem (Jer. 15:3-4).

It got worse! Manasseh's son (and Josiah's father), Amon:

> ...did what was evil in the sight of the LORD, as Manasseh his father had done. He walked in all the way in which his father walked and served the idols that his father served and worshipped them. He abandoned the LORD, the God of his fathers, and did not walk in the way of the LORD (2 Kings 21:20-22)...

...and he was assassinated in his own house (2 Kings 21:23). Nevertheless, even with such a calamitous upbringing, we know that Josiah himself – astonishingly – although he was only 'eight years old when he began to reign' (2 Kings 22:1), swam against the prevailing wind and tide, and:

> ...did what was right in the eyes of the LORD and walked in all the way of David his father, and... did not turn aside to the right or to the left (2 Kings 22:2).

But there was even more to the young man (or, rather, to start with, boy) than that. We know that he was a consistent, fervent reformer. One event stands out. The men who were repairing the temple (2 Kings 22:3-7) came across the book of the law – which, evidently, had been lost. That shows how bad things had become in Judah at the time! The book of the law was brought to the king, and Shaphan read it to him (2 Kings 22:8-10). The king, deeply affected by the words he was hearing (2 Kings 22:11), issued a pressing command:

> Go, inquire of the LORD for me, and for the people, and for all Judah, concerning the words of this book that has been found. For great is the wrath of the LORD that is kindled

Responsibilities

against us, because our fathers have not obeyed the words of this book, to do according to all that is written concerning us (2 Kings 22:13).

God used Huldah the prophetess to reply to the king:

> Thus says the LORD, the God of Israel: 'Tell the man who sent you to me: Thus says the LORD, Behold, I will bring disaster upon this place and upon its inhabitants, all the words of the book that the king of Judah has read. Because they have forsaken me and have made offerings to other gods, that they might provoke me to anger with all the work of their hands, therefore my wrath will be kindled against this place, and it will not be quenched. But to the king of Judah, who sent you to inquire of the LORD, thus shall you say to him: Thus says the LORD, the God of Israel: Regarding the words that you have heard, because your heart was penitent, and you humbled yourself before the LORD, when you heard how I spoke against this place and against its inhabitants, that they should become a desolation and a curse, and you have torn your clothes and wept before me, I also have heard you, declares the LORD. Therefore, behold, I will gather you to your fathers, and you shall be gathered to your grave in peace, and your eyes shall not see all the disaster that I will bring upon this place' (2 Kings 22:15-20).

Clearly, God had determined that the kingdom of Judah, because of its betrayal of the covenant, was unavoidably heading for disaster, but he would spare Josiah himself. *And Josiah knew both these facts.* Both points must be stressed: Judah was doomed beyond recall, but Josiah himself was safe. If ever a man had cause – on both counts – to relax, ease up and coast all the way, that man was Josiah. He could breathe a huge sigh of relief on his own behalf, and excuse himself from further concern since God had determined to take Judah, because of their former sins, into exile – whatever Josiah, himself, might do. Sit back, sit tight, and wait!

But no! He did not take Hezekiah's line (2 Kings 20:16-19). Look at Josiah's response:

> Then the king sent, and all the elders of Judah and Jerusalem were gathered to him. And the king went up to the house of

Responsibilities

the LORD, and with him all the men of Judah and all the inhabitants of Jerusalem and the priests and the prophets, all the people, both small and great. And he read in their hearing all the words of the book of the covenant that had been found in the house of the LORD. And the king stood by the pillar and made a covenant before the LORD, to walk after the LORD and to keep his commandments and his testimonies and his statutes with all his heart and all his soul, to perform the words of this covenant that were written in this book. And all the people joined in the covenant (2 Kings 23:1-3).

Despite knowing the promise of personal safety and the prediction of inevitable disaster for the nation, the king acted as though the calamity could be averted: he started by making the people renew the covenant according to the book of the law.

And that's not all. The king gave orders to rid the temple of every last vestige of Baal and Asherah worship, along with all the rest of the idolatrous trash which had accumulated over the years. He abolished all the evil practices, all the corruptions, which had defiled Jerusalem. And so it went on. Josiah ensured that a root-and-branch reform of Judaism was put in hand; all the idolatrous priests and 'the male cult prostitutes' were got rid of; and he showed his contempt for all the evil of which the people of Judah had grown so fond. In a dramatic, widespread clean-sweep, he pushed hoary age and tradition aside; nothing stopped him. He accomplished a thorough-going reform according to the law of the covenant (2 Kings 23:4-20). Despite knowing that there was no hope, he did not let up before the reform was as complete as he could make it.

Positively, he showed respect for the interred remains of the faithful prophets who had denounced the altar of Jeroboam the son of Nebat (2 Kings 23:17-18), and he reinstated the Passover according to the law, commanding the people:

> Keep the Passover to the LORD your God, as it is written in this book of the covenant (2 Kings 23:21).

So much so, God awarded Josiah this accolade:

Responsibilities

> No such Passover had been kept since the days of the judges who judged Israel, or during all the days of the kings of Israel or of the kings of Judah. But in the eighteenth year of King Josiah this Passover was kept to the LORD in Jerusalem. Moreover, Josiah put away the mediums and the necromancers and the household gods and the idols and all the abominations that were seen in the land of Judah and in Jerusalem, that he might establish the words of the law that were written in the book that Hilkiah the priest found in the house of the LORD. Before him there was no king like him, who turned to the LORD with all his heart and with all his soul and with all his might, according to all the law of Moses, nor did any like him arise after him (2 Kings 23:22-25).

But, as the Scripture immediately goes on to state, despite all Josiah's sweeping reforms, God still did not turn from his stated intention to take Judah into captivity:

> Still the LORD did not turn from the burning of his great wrath, by which his anger was kindled against Judah, because of all the provocations with which Manasseh had provoked him. And the LORD said: 'I will remove Judah also out of my sight, as I have removed Israel, and I will cast off this city that I have chosen, Jerusalem, and the house of which I said, My name shall be there' (2 Kings 23:26-27).

I underline my point. Josiah was exceedingly zealous in his obedience to God's word, even though he knew God's purpose was to deliver him, personally, while putting an end to Judah, at least for seventy years. The king did not allow the assurance of his own personal deliverance, nor the immensity of the task before him, nor the impossibility of long-term success – indeed, the absolute certainty of failure and disaster – to deter him. No wonder, then, as we have seen, God's epitaph for Josiah stands in Scripture:

> He did what was right in the eyes of the LORD and walked in all the way of David his father, and he did not turn aside to the right or to the left (2 Kings 22:2).

And the same goes for the days of the new covenant. As we saw earlier, Paul knew what would happen at Ephesus after his departure:

Responsibilities

I know that after my departure fierce wolves will come in among you, not sparing the flock; and from among your own selves will arise men speaking twisted things, to draw away the disciples after them. Therefore be alert, remembering that for three years I did not cease night or day to admonish every one with tears (Acts 20:29-31).

Moreover, as we also saw, this was only one example of his dire predictions about the course of this age. My purpose in referring to this again is to argue that despite his conviction (rather, his certain knowledge) of impending apostasy, of the inevitable undoing of so much of his work, Paul did not throw in the towel; he pressed on, even in face of certain disappointment. He continued to spend his life travelling, writing and preaching, doing all he could to advance the gospel, rejoicing in that advance even when he was in prison, and others were seeing the success (Phil. 1:12-18). His final recorded-words were no idle boast:

> I am already being poured out as a drink offering, and the time of my departure [that is, death] has come. I have fought the good fight, I have finished the race, I have kept the faith (2 Tim. 4:6-7).

And, taking the point to the highest level, Christ himself saw no contradiction between his conviction – his certain knowledge – that absolute power was in God his Father's hand, and knowing the impotence of men – the utter powerlessness of mere men to bring about God's purpose – yet still he required his people to work for him. While asserting that he (alone) has 'all power', yet still he commanded mere mortals to labour for him,[14] even though the task is way beyond them:

> All authority in heaven and on earth has been given to me. Go therefore and make disciples of all nations, baptising them in the name of the Father and of the Son and of the Holy Spirit, teaching them to observe all that I have commanded you. And behold, I am with you always, to the end of the age (Matt. 28:18-20).

---

[14] See 'Our Privilege and Duty' in my *The Glorious*.

Responsibilities

> Go into all the world and proclaim the gospel to the whole creation. Whoever believes and is baptised will be saved, but whoever does not believe will be condemned (Mark 16:15-16).

> Repentance for the forgiveness of sins should be proclaimed in his name to all nations, beginning from Jerusalem (Luke 24:47).

> You will receive power when the Holy Spirit has come upon you, and you will be my witnesses in Jerusalem and in all Judea and Samaria, and to the end of the earth (Acts 1:8).

The task beyond them? I am thinking not merely (what a word!) of the size of the task – of reaching the world; the very nature of the task, in itself, is absolutely beyond human power. Only the sovereign Spirit can regenerate sinners; man is utterly impotent (Ezek. 36:26; John 1:11-13; 3:3-8; 2 Cor. 4:3-6; Eph. 2:1-5; Jas. 1:18; 1 Pet. 1:3; 1 John 5:11). Even so, Christ saw no paralysing dilemma here: God is sovereign; men are incapable; but weak men are to carry out the impossible; and in and through it all, God will accomplish his purpose. God delights – is 'pleased' – to use weakness to accomplish his sovereign will. As Paul put it:

> The word of the cross is folly to those who are perishing, but to us who are being saved it is the power of God... Where is the one who is wise? Where is the scribe? Where is the debater of this age? Has not God made foolish the wisdom of the world? For since, in the wisdom of God, the world did not know God through wisdom, it pleased God through the folly of what we preach [or, the folly of preaching] to save those who believe. For Jews demand signs and Greeks seek wisdom, but we preach Christ crucified, a stumbling block to Jews and folly to Gentiles, but to those who are called, both Jews and Greeks, Christ the power of God and the wisdom of God. For the foolishness of God is wiser than men, and the weakness of God is stronger than men (1 Cor. 1:18-25).

As he had already explained:

> Christ [sent] me... to preach the gospel... not with words of eloquent wisdom, lest the cross of Christ be emptied of its power (1 Cor. 1:17).

Responsibilities

And as he went on to tell the Corinthians:

> I, when I came to you, brothers, did not come proclaiming to you the testimony of God with lofty speech or wisdom. For I decided [determined] to know nothing among you except Jesus Christ and him crucified. And I was with you in weakness and in fear and much trembling, and my speech and my message were not in plausible words of wisdom, but in demonstration of the Spirit and of power, so that your faith might not rest in the wisdom of men but in the power of God (1 Cor. 2:1-5).

But, of course, this spiritual wisdom is the only true wisdom; it is dismissed as nonsense by the world, but wisdom – true wisdom – it really is:

> Yet among the mature we do impart wisdom, although it is not a wisdom of this age or of the rulers of this age, who are doomed to pass away. But we impart a secret and hidden wisdom of God, which God decreed before the ages for our glory (1 Cor. 2:6-7).

In short, the apostle experienced the reality of what the prophet had stated centuries before:

> Not by might, nor by power, but by my Spirit, says the LORD of hosts (Zech. 4:6).

And the same must go for us. God will not allow anyone to take the glory (Isa. 42:8; 48:11). As Paul told the Corinthians:

> [The] base things of the world, and things which are despised, has God chosen, indeed, and things which are not, to bring to nought things that are: That no flesh should glory in his presence (1 Cor. 1:28-29).

Notwithstanding the calamitous rise of Christendom and the immense damage it is causing during 'these latter days', God is still gathering his elect. Nothing – nothing – can thwart God's purpose in Christ. As he himself declared:

> I have other sheep that are not of this fold. I must bring them also, and they will listen to my voice (John 10:16; see also John 11:52).

Christ was declaring that the elect (both Jew and Gentile; here, particularly the latter) must be saved; they will be saved; that is, they will hear his call in the gospel, and hear it effectively; they will listen to it, they will be persuaded, they will turn from their sin, they will come to him, they will be brought to trust him, listen to all he has to say, and act upon it in obedience.

Of course, even the elect – who, by nature, as all men, are dead in sin (Eph. 2:13) – cannot believe unless, by God the Father's grace and power, the Spirit regenerates them (John 1:11-13; 3:3-8):

> You refuse to come to me that you may have life (John 5:40).

> No one can come to me unless the Father who sent me draws him. And I will raise him up on the last day. It is written in the prophets: 'And they will all be taught by God'. Everyone who has heard and learned from the Father comes to me (John 6:44-45).

Such is Christ's verdict of man. But he was explicit in his assurance:

> All that the Father gives me will come to me, and whoever comes to me I will never cast out (John 6:37).

The point once again: the task is beyond human ingenuity. Nevertheless, the believer must go on in obedience to his Master's call.

But this does not exhaust the believer's responsibilities.

Believers must be careful to maintain their separation from the world

That believers must be separate from the world, is, I assert, a biblical truism. It must be so: *ekklēsia*, called-out ones, called out from the world.

Let us start with the fundamental position. As John put it:

> We know that we are from God, and the whole world lies in the power of the evil one (1 John 5:19).

Responsibilities

That was true nearly 2000 years ago, and nothing has changed. 'The whole world' was utterly under Satan's power, evil, in John's day. Indeed, as he put it, the world, society, culture rested in – 'lies in' – being under Satan's control. Note also the clear separation which John drew between – believers – the *ekklēsia* – and the rest. I talk of 'separation'. What about distinction, demarcation, disconnection, division, detachment, disengagement, disentanglement? Why did God send his Son into this hostile world? As Paul explained, God sent his Son so that Christ might give:

> ...himself for our [that is, the elect's] sins to deliver us from the present evil age, according to the will of our God and Father (Gal. 1:4).

As Paul said – again, nearly 2000 years ago – Christ died to redeem the elect from – out of – this 'present evil age'. Paul used *exaireō*, literally 'to take out'.

The world, the culture, was evil two millennia ago; it has been evil since Adam's fall; it was evil in Noah's day; it was evil at Babel; it was evil in Christ's day. In short, the world is always this 'present evil age'. It can be nothing else.

I agree that when sufficient numbers are truly converted, a society will to a certain extent conform to some of the ethics of the gospel. (Do not miss the deliberate vagueness of that statement!) But in truth, conformity is a far cry from regeneration (John 1:12-13; 3:3-8), leading to conversion (Acts 2:38-39; 3:19; 16:31; 17:30-311; 2 Cor. 5:17; Gal. 6:15), leading to transformation into Christ's likeness (Rom. 8:28-30; 12:2; 2 Cor. 3:17-18; Eph. 4:12-16; Phil. 3:10; Col. 3:10; 1 John 2:6; 4:17)! All men and women are either in Adam or in Christ (Rom. 5:12-19; 1 Cor. 15:22,45). Society is always – always – wicked. It may or may not become more or less religious, but it is always hostile to God (Rom. 8:7; Jas. 4:4). A religious culture is still a wicked culture. Christendom is a 'Christianised' culture, but it is evil. Christendom encourages conformity, but as for regeneration and progressive

Responsibilities

sanctification leading to Christ's likeness, it is powerless, and worse.[15]

Scripture plainly teaches that the natural man is in the world, and he is of the world, whereas the believer, while he is still in the world, but most decidedly he is not of the world.

Although they find themselves tangled in the web of Christendom, believers, as well as adhering to the new covenant, and doing what they can to advance the gospel in the world, must learn from Israel's dreadful failure, and, being determined not to be buddies with the world, refuse to copy the bad example Israel set. Indeed, believers must be careful to maintain their separation from the world. James could not have expressed himself more strongly:

> You adulterous people! Do you not know that friendship with the world is enmity with God? Therefore whoever wishes to be a friend of the world makes himself an enemy of God (Jas. 4:4).

Nor did John fail to make the point:

> Do not love the world or the things in the world. If anyone loves the world, the love of the Father is not in him. For all that is in the world – the desires of the flesh and the desires of the eyes and pride of life – is not from the Father but is from the world. And the world is passing away along with its desires, but whoever does the will of God abides forever (1 John 2:15-17).

Indeed, separation was Paul's major point in 1 Corinthians 10:1-14. The blunt fact is that when the covenant people – Israel in the old covenant, believers in the new – dabble with paganism, it is tantamount to idolatry (1 Cor. 10:14).[16] It is

---

[15] See my 'To Be Transformed' on my sermonaudio.com page, and on YouTube. See also Rick Peterson: 'Transformed not just Reformed' on his sermonaudio.com page.

[16] Charles Ellicott: 'These words show that through all the previous argument and warning, [Paul] had in view the particular dangers arising from their [that is, the Corinthians'] contact with the heathen world, and especially the partaking in the sacrificial feasts... Because

Responsibilities

destructive of God's covenant – the Mosaic for Israel, the new for believers. Israel flouted God's repeated commands, they trampled on their own voluntary vow (Ex. 19:8). Remember, they had freely given their word that they would serve and obey God in all that he said to them. Even so, again and again they turned to pagans and paganism, playing fast and loose with the covenant (Hos. 8:1). Believers must not copy this disastrous example. Although it is well-nigh impossible to avoid Christendom altogether, believers must steer clear of its tentacles:

> Jesus... suffered outside the gate in order to sanctify the people through his own blood. Therefore let us go to him outside the camp and bear the reproach he endured. For here we have no lasting city, but we seek the city that is to come (Heb. 13:12-14).

Where is Christ? 'Outside the camp'. Where must believers be? 'Outside the camp'.

> Do not be unequally yoked with unbelievers. For what partnership has righteousness with lawlessness? Or what fellowship has light with darkness? What accord has Christ with Belial? Or what portion does a believer share with an unbeliever? What agreement has the temple of God with idols? For we are the temple of the living God; as God said: 'I will make my dwelling among them and walk among them, and I will be their God, and they shall be my people. Therefore go out from their midst, and be separate from them, says the Lord, and touch no unclean thing; then I will welcome you, and I will be a father to you, and you shall be sons and daughters to me, says the Lord Almighty' (2 Cor. 6:14-18).

> Come out of her [that is, Babylon], my people, lest you take part in her sins, lest you share in her plagues (Rev. 18:4).

And there is yet another responsibility laid upon believers.

---

they are [God's] "beloved" he had written thus to them. Because God is a faithful God – because he makes it possible for you to escape these dangers and sins – flee from idolatry! Do not be trying [to see] how near you can get to it, but rather how far you can get from it' (Charles Ellicott: *Commentary*, slightly edited linguistically).

Believers must shine as warning lights in a dangerous darkness

As Paul put it to the Philippians:

> ...that you may be blameless and innocent, children of God without blemish in the midst of a crooked and twisted generation, among whom you shine as lights in the world, holding fast to the word of life (Phil. 2:15-16).

Notice that Paul had no need to command his readers to 'shine as lights in the world, holding fast to the word of life'; nor did he do so; he simply assumed that they were doing it – he took it for granted, if you like. Apparently, every believer in those early days knew that being a believer meant that you would be one of those who 'shine as lights in the world, holding fast to the word of life'. We, today, need to recover this spirit, this assumption, this taken-for-granted.

After all, Christ could not have made it plainer:

> You are the light of the world. A city set on a hill cannot be hidden. Nor do people light a lamp and put it under a basket, but on a stand, and it gives light to all in the house. In the same way, let your light shine before others, so that they may see your good works and give glory to your Father who is in heaven (Matt. 5:14-16).

Believers are to be known, as their Master was (John 8:12; 9:5), as lights, shining by word and deed. As he told them:

> The light [Christ, himself] is among you for a little while longer. Walk while you have the light, lest darkness overtake you. The one who walks in the darkness does not know where he is going. While you have the light, believe in the light, that you may become sons of light (John 12:35-36).

A light, a lamp? What do you do with a light, a lamp? It may be obvious, but we need to hear the obvious. Christ twice made the point, and Luke recorded both occasions:

> No one after lighting a lamp covers it with a jar or puts it under a bed, but puts it on a stand, so that those who enter may see the light (Luke 8:16; see also, Mark 4:21).

Responsibilities

No one after lighting a lamp puts it in a cellar or under a basket, but on a stand, so that those who enter may see the light (Luke 11:33).

Two thousand years ago, the light in question in Philippians 2:15-16 would have been the stars, or a flaming torch of some sort. Today, the illustration can be extended to warning lights familiar to us all – lighthouses, traffic signals, electronic equipment, warning indicators in cars, and such like. Here is the passage again:

...that you may be blameless and innocent, children of God without blemish in the midst of a crooked and twisted generation, among whom you shine as lights in the world, holding fast to the word of life (Phil. 2:15-16).

There are two connected issues here: believers are to be shining lights by holding to, and holding out, the word of God. They are to be both warning and guiding lights.

In other words, believers must, as lighthouses, warn of dangerous reefs and rocks, while at the same time, welcome threatened mariners into a safe haven. In short, believers have to confront those in a dangerous darkness,[17] doing what they can to stop them in their wild career',[18] and, at the same time, encourage them to come to safety.

Take confrontation. The prophets confronted. Christ confronted. The apostles confronted. Even though we are not in that class, nevertheless we have to shine; that is, we have to confront. Doing nothing is doing something.[19]

---

[17] See my *To Confront*.

[18] Borrowed from a hymn by John Newton (1725 – 1807): 'In evil long I took delight,/Unawed by shame or fear;/Till a new object struck my sight,/And stopped my wild career'.

[19] Take the Columbia Shuttle disaster in 2003; the capsule disintegrated on re-entering the earth's atmosphere, with the death of the seven astronauts. But all the ground-agencies knew that something had gone wrong right at the start of the mission: some heat-protecting foam had come loose on lift-off, and hit one of the wings of the re-entry craft. There was uncertainty about the damage – if any, how

Let me probe this. Note Paul's reference to 'a crooked and twisted generation'; believers have to be:

> ...blameless and innocent, children of God without blemish *in the midst of a crooked and twisted generation*.

In choosing this phrase to make his point – 'in the midst of a crooked and twisted generation' – the apostle was not thinking primarily of the believer's witness in a hostile, pagan world of rank unbelievers; rather, he was going back to the time of Moses, who, towards the end of his life, when he was addressing Israel, declared that the Jews in their disobedience:

> ...have dealt corruptly with [God]; they are no longer his children because they are blemished; they are a crooked and twisted generation (Deut. 32:5).

'They are a crooked and twisted generation'. Who were the 'they'? Not pagans, not Moabites, not Egyptians, but Jews, the professing people of God under the old covenant. It was Israel that was 'the... crooked and twisted generation'.

And Peter used the same imagery when he appealed to his hearers on the day of Pentecost. He was addressing Jews (Acts 2:5,14,22,29,36), and his words were blunt, unvarnished: 'Save yourselves from this crooked generation' (Acts 2:40). 'This crooked generation'. Peter was thinking of the Jews. Gentiles did not come into the picture until Acts 10.

'This crooked generation' – as used by Moses and Peter – clearly referred to the mass of unbelieving Jews; as used by Paul it probably referred to the Jewish teachers, the *pseudadelphoi*, and their followers who were infiltrating themselves and their false gospel into the *ekklēsia*. The present

---

much, how serious – this has caused. After much debate and analysis – but almost all done in the dark – the top management decided that all was well. Several in the lower ranks, however, were very disturbed. Even so, nobody said anything – management protocol, their own job security, making them keep silence. Hence the disaster, and all the conscience-racking which followed. Not to speak is not to do nothing.

Responsibilities

application is patent: in 'the last days' faithful believers need to shine as lighthouses, beaming their warning light to Christendom, professors of Christ who, like the unfaithful Jews in Moses' day, were disobedient to the old covenant, and, like the *pseudadelphoi* in Paul's day, were disobedient to the new covenant, and tampering with it; in short, to 'a crooked and twisted generation'. Of course believers have to confront pagans, rank unbelievers, but they are called especially to confront Christendom, professing believers who are drifting away from the new covenant;[20] in-house, as it were. That is where the buck starts!

Alongside that, believers must shine out to Christendom-believers, encouraging them to come into the safe harbour – that is, away from Christendom, and back to the new covenant.[21]

We live in an effeminate day; confrontation is not liked. C.H.Spurgeon, developing some words by Thomas Manton – 'There is a time for the trumpet as well as the pipe' – had something to say about this – and we would do well to listen to him:

> We must sometimes sound an alarm; we should be traitors to men's souls and to our Master if we always piped to dulcet music. He who is always comforting...[22] people will find no comfort when he is called to answer for it before his God another day. Many souls need Boanerges [sons of thunder, using Christ's term (Mark 3:17)] more than Barnabas [son of encouragement (Acts 4:36)], thunder more than dew. By many who think themselves great judges, the trumpet-discourse is judged to be too harsh, and the piper is commended for his pleasant strains; and yet the Lord may distribute the praise and the blame very differently. My heart, do not be always craving for soft music. Be willing to be startled and stimulated. Life is

---

[20] See also Matt. 17; Luke 9:41.
[21] A difficult paragraph. All believers are in some sort of Christendom, but most are unaware of it. It is impossible to escape Christendom altogether.
[22] I have omitted 'his'.

Responsibilities

a conflict, and you need battle music to keep you up to fighting pitch. Let those who dance with the world [for my purpose, I would add 'Christendom' – DG] pay the pipers who play to them [soothing notes regarding Christendom – DG]; as for you, give your ear to the King's trumpeters.[23]

The challenge, the responsibility, the privilege laid on every believer is... what? To be one of 'the King's trumpeters'!

And, if I might so term it, what is our greatest responsibility?

Believers must remain faithful to God and his truth in the midst of apostasy, even when apostasy is widespread and prolonged, and close at hand

This follows directly from the previous point. Shining to 'a crooked and twisted generation', being a warning light, sending out a beacon to direct mariners into the right, the safe channel, means that believers need to be thoroughly reliable, faithful, trustworthy, and their witness needs to be such. They must 'hold... fast to the word of life' (Phil. 2:16). They have to be devoted to the new covenant, holding fast to Scripture. Mariners looking for a safe harbour need to be sure that the light which warns them of rocks, or shows them the way to safety, really is telling the truth, and that they can stake their life upon it. The apostle laid down the principle:

> It is required of stewards that they be found faithful (1 Cor. 4:2).

> Be watchful, stand firm in the faith (1 Cor. 16:13).

> Let your manner of life be worthy of the gospel of Christ, so that whether I come and see you or am absent, I may hear of you that you are standing firm in one spirit, with one mind striving side by side for the faith of the gospel, and not frightened in anything by your opponents. This is a clear sign to them of their destruction, but of your salvation, and that from God (Phil. 1:27-28).

---

[23] C.H.Spurgeon: *Flowers from a Puritan's Garden*.

Responsibilities

Therefore, my brothers, whom I love and long for, my joy and crown, stand firm thus in the Lord, my beloved (Phil. 4:1).

'Faithful' and 'stand firm' are the key words. Believers have to be faithful, reliable, trustworthy, dependable, standing firm, persevering, standing upright; men and women of integrity. Faithful lights are needed on dark nights.

The lighthouse has to be a fixture. The position of the stars is absolutely reliable. If lighthouse-keepers move the light on a whim or according to local fashion, or if a traveller depends on a wandering meteor, disaster ensues. The whole notion is of sureness, reliability, fixity.[24] James spoke of God as:

...the Father of lights, with whom there is no variation or shadow due to change (Jas. 1:17).

The prophet had recorded God's declaration about himself:

I the LORD do not change (Mal. 3:6).

And long before, Balaam had stated it:

God is not man, that he should lie, or a son of man, that he should change his mind. Has he said, and will he not do it? Or has he spoken, and will he not fulfil it? (Num. 23:19).

As their Father, so believers must be – shining with 'no variation or shadow due to change', not being as the wicked, 'double-minded... unstable in all [their] ways' (Jas. 1:8; see also Jas. 4:8); they must never be 'ignorant and unstable' (2 Pet. 3:16; see also 2 Pet. 2:14), 'wandering stars' (Jude 13).

In short, believers have to be noted for their reliability, for their integrity, their stability, that they hold forth the truth and they stick to it, that they remain faithful. And never was faithfulness to the gospel more important than today. For this is a day marked, in general, by appallingly-weak doctrinal knowledge, and a signal lack of interest in doctrine, coupled with an

---

[24] Cornish wrecking (as set out, say, in *Jamaica Inn* by Daphne du Maurier) is probably a myth, but the apocryphal image shows what happens when lights are false.

Responsibilities

increasing tendency to regard sin as sin only when it becomes public, or when it results in blatantly-sinful acts.[25] Concern for doctrinal and practical detail counts far less than a sense of well-being. Today's lighthouse-keepers give the impression of being a well-meaning, happy bunch, but whether the light they beam out is accurate, reliable, trustworthy – that is the question. Mariners in the storm would be well-advised to bear it in mind!

Believers need to worry less about their enjoyment, and get to grips with obeying Peter's injunction (the KJV sticking literally to the Greek):

> Gird up the loins of your mind (1 Pet. 1:13).

That's it! Good feelings are good, but only if the mind is awake and awake to the truth. Believers are living in a hostile world – paganism and Christendom – and adherence to truth is an essential; it is not an option, a luxury, an add-on for the few. Interest in doctrine – deliberately to understate it – is not a hobby for a few believing-nerds. Every believer is to be a shining light in a dark world. When all around gives way, gives ground, the believer must be faithful, and about his Master's business. As Christ declared:

> But concerning that day and hour [that is, of his return] no one knows, not even the angels of heaven, nor the Son, but the Father only. For as were the days of Noah, so will be the coming of the Son of Man. For as in those days before the flood they were eating and drinking, marrying and giving in marriage, until the day when Noah entered the ark, and they were unaware until the flood came and swept them all away, so will be the coming of the Son of Man. Then two men will be in the field; one will be taken and one left. Two women will be grinding at the mill; one will be taken and one left. Therefore, stay awake, for you do not know on what day your Lord is coming. But know this, that if the master of the house had known in what part of the night the thief was coming, he would have stayed awake and would not have let his house be broken into. Therefore you also must be ready, for the Son of

---

[25] Louis Mazzini: 'These things only become wrong when people know about them' (talking to Sibella, in *Kind Hearts and Coronets*).

Responsibilities

Man is coming at an hour you do not expect. Who then is the faithful and wise servant, whom his master has set over his household, to give them their food at the proper time? (Matt. 24:36-45).

And:

For it will be like a man going on a journey, who called his servants and entrusted to them his property. To one he gave five talents, to another two, to another one, to each according to his ability. Then he went away. He who had received the five talents went at once and traded with them, and he made five talents more. So also he who had the two talents made two talents more. But he who had received the one talent went and dug in the ground and hid his master's money. Now after a long time the master of those servants came and settled accounts with them. And he who had received the five talents came forward, bringing five talents more, saying: 'Master, you delivered to me five talents; here, I have made five talents more'. His master said to him: 'Well done, good and faithful servant. You have been faithful over a little; I will set you over much. Enter into the joy of your master'. And he also who had the two talents came forward, saying: 'Master, you delivered to me two talents; here, I have made two talents more'. His master said to him: 'Well done, good and faithful servant. You have been faithful over a little; I will set you over much. Enter into the joy of your master'. He also who had received the one talent came forward, saying: 'Master, I knew you to be a hard man, reaping where you did not sow, and gathering where you scattered no seed, so I was afraid, and I went and hid your talent in the ground. Here, you have what is yours'. But his master answered him: 'You wicked and slothful servant! You knew that I reap where I have not sown and gather where I scattered no seed? Then you ought to have invested my money with the bankers, and at my coming I should have received what was my own with interest. So take the talent from him and give it to him who has the ten talents. For to everyone who has will more be given, and he will have an abundance. But from the one who has not, even what he has will be taken away. And cast the worthless servant into the outer darkness. In that place there will be weeping and gnashing of teeth' (Matt. 25:14-30).

As the closing book of Scripture stresses:

Responsibilities

[Christ's enemies] will make war on the Lamb, and the Lamb will conquer them, for he is Lord of lords and King of kings, and those with him are called and chosen and faithful (Rev. 17:14).

'Faithful' is the word.

APPENDICES

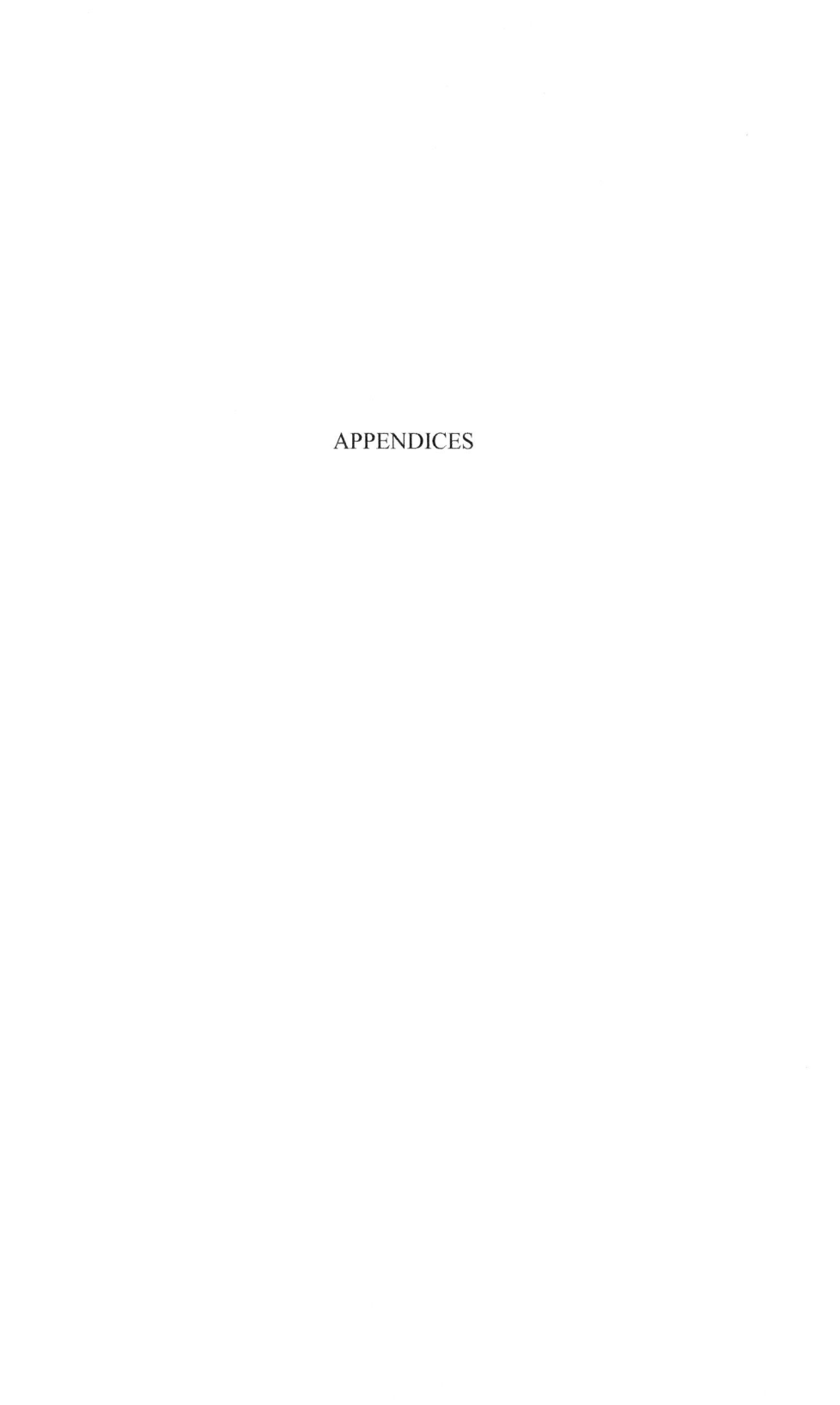

Appendix 1: Daniel 2:44

Nebuchadnezzar had a dream in which he saw a colossal statue shattered by a small stone. This vision proved beyond the wit of the wise men of Babylon to interpret. Indeed, the king had put the magicians to the test by demanding that they tell him what he had seen in his dream *before* giving its meaning. The magicians failed on both counts. Under God, however, Daniel was able to do both – to confirm the king's dream, and then to interpret the vision. He explained that God – the God of Judah, Daniel's God, the one true God – was going to destroy a succession of world-kingdoms by setting up his own kingdom, an everlasting kingdom:

> In the days of those kings the God of heaven will set up a kingdom that shall never be destroyed, nor shall the kingdom be left to another people. It shall break in pieces all these kingdoms and bring them to an end, and it shall stand forever (Dan. 2:44).

Opinions are divided. Virtually all are agreed that the vision refers to Christ (Ps. 118:22; Isa. 8:14-15; 28:16; Matt. 21:42; Mark 12:10-11; Luke 20:17-18; Acts 4:11; Eph. 2:20; 1 Pet. 2:4-8) and the triumph of his kingdom. But it is in the 'how' and 'when' where the differences of view lie.

Here is my view. Imperial Rome fell in the early 5th century. But it did not fall because of the gospel. It fell because of paganism – both within the empire and in the pagan hordes under Alaric. Nebuchadnezzar's vision has nothing to say about this. In addition, patently the vision does not speak in terms of a steady advance, leading to a glorious kingdom. There is nothing gradual or secret about it at all. It is not a process. Quite the opposite! The vision describes a shattering – a sudden, devastating smashing – of the kingdoms of the world, an explosion, which blasts them into smithereens, leaving Christ's kingdom standing as the sole, eternal kingdom. The only event to which this can refer must be:

Appendix 1:Daniel 2:44

...Christ... at his [second] coming... Then comes the end, when he delivers the kingdom to God the Father after destroying every rule and every authority and power. For he must reign until he has put all his enemies under his feet. The last enemy to be destroyed is death. For 'God has put all things in subjection under his feet'... When all things are subjected to him, then the Son himself will also be subjected to him who put all things in subjection under him, that God may be all in all (1 Cor. 15:23-28).

And:

The seventh angel blew his trumpet, and there were loud voices in heaven, saying: 'The kingdom of the world has become the kingdom of our Lord and of his Christ, and he shall reign forever and ever' (Rev. 11:15).

This clearly harks back to Daniel's own vision of the four beasts when:

...the Ancient of Days came, and judgment was given for the saints of the Most High, and the time came when the saints possessed the kingdom.
Thus he said: 'As for the fourth beast, there shall be a fourth kingdom on earth, which shall be different from all the kingdoms, and it shall devour the whole earth, and trample it down, and break it to pieces. As for the ten horns, out of this kingdom ten kings shall arise, and another shall arise after them; he shall be different from the former ones, and shall put down three kings. He shall speak words against the Most High, and shall wear out the saints of the Most High, and shall think to change the times and the law; and they shall be given into his hand for a time, times, and half a time. But the court shall sit in judgment, and his dominion shall be taken away, to be consumed and destroyed to the end. And the kingdom and the dominion and the greatness of the kingdoms under the whole heaven shall be given to the people of the saints of the Most High; his kingdom shall be an everlasting kingdom, and all dominions shall serve and obey him' (Dan. 7:22-27).

In other words, as I understand the vision, Christ, in his second coming, will, in an instant, put an end to all earthly kingdoms, and establish his own, everlasting, kingdom.

And, as I understand it, this is what Christ predicted:

Appendix 1:Daniel 2:44

Jerusalem will be trampled underfoot by the Gentiles, until the times of the Gentiles are fulfilled. And there will be signs in sun and moon and stars, and on the earth distress of nations in perplexity because of the roaring of the sea and the waves, people fainting with fear and with foreboding of what is coming on the world. For the powers of the heavens will be shaken. And then they will see the Son of Man coming in a cloud with power and great glory. Now when these things begin to take place, straighten up and raise your heads, because your redemption is drawing near (Luke 21:24-28).

And John saw this in the Revelation:

Then the seventh angel blew his trumpet, and there were loud voices in heaven, saying: 'The kingdom of the world has become the kingdom of our Lord and of his Christ, and he shall reign forever and ever'. And the twenty-four elders who sit on their thrones before God fell on their faces and worshipped God, saying: 'We give thanks to you, Lord God Almighty, who is and who was, for you have taken your great power and begun to reign. The nations raged, but your wrath came, and the time for the dead to be judged, and for rewarding your servants, the prophets and saints, and those who fear your name, both small and great, and for destroying the destroyers of the earth'. Then God's temple in heaven was opened, and the ark of his covenant was seen within his temple. There were flashes of lightning, rumblings, peals of thunder, an earthquake, and heavy hail (Rev. 11:15-19).

Then I saw heaven opened, and behold, a white horse! The one sitting on it is called Faithful and True, and in righteousness he judges and makes war. His eyes are like a flame of fire, and on his head are many diadems, and he has a name written that no one knows but himself. He is clothed in a robe dipped in blood, and the name by which he is called is The Word of God. And the armies of heaven, arrayed in fine linen, white and pure, were following him on white horses. From his mouth comes a sharp sword with which to strike down the nations, and he will rule them with a rod of iron. He will tread the winepress of the fury of the wrath of God the Almighty. On his robe and on his thigh he has a name written, King of kings and Lord of lords. Then I saw an angel standing in the sun, and with a loud voice he called to all the birds that fly directly overhead: 'Come, gather for the great supper of

Appendix 1:Daniel 2:44

God, to eat the flesh of kings, the flesh of captains, the flesh of mighty men, the flesh of horses and their riders, and the flesh of all men, both free and slave, both small and great'. And I saw the beast and the kings of the earth with their armies gathered to make war against him who was sitting on the horse and against his army. And the beast was captured, and with it the false prophet who in its presence had done the signs by which he deceived those who had received the mark of the beast and those who worshipped its image. These two were thrown alive into the lake of fire that burns with sulphur. And the rest were slain by the sword that came from the mouth of him who was sitting on the horse, and all the birds were gorged with their flesh (Rev. 19:11-21).

* * *

Let Samuel Prideaux Tregelles set out his interpretation of Daniel 2:44:

Now, what does the stone so falling upon the feet of the image symbolise? It has been sometimes thought that it alludes to grace, or to the spread of the gospel; but surely if the very words of the Scripture be followed, we shall see that destroying judgment on Gentile [that is, pagan – DG] power is here spoken of, and not any gradual diffusion of the knowledge of grace... The whole image is destroyed as it were with one crash.

Now, our Lord [Jesus Christ himself] speaks of himself as the 'stone', and makes reference, or direct citation of, several passages in the Old Testament in which he had been so designated. Thus in Matthew 21:42,44: 'Did you never read in the scriptures, The stone which the builders rejected, the same is become the head of the corner: this is the Lord's doing, and it is marvellous in our eyes?... And whosoever shall fall on this stone shall be broken; but on whomsoever it shall fall, it will grind him to powder'. Our Lord here cites from Psalm 118, and alludes to the mention made in Isaiah 8 to the stone on which Israel has stumbled and been broken; and he likewise clearly refers to the destroying judgment which takes place when the stone, now exalted at the head of the corner, falls thus upon the fabric of Gentile power – 'it will grind him to powder'.

'The stone' must be taken as a definite appellation of our Lord. We see this from Psalm 118:22; Isaiah 8:14; 28:16, Acts

Appendix 1:Daniel 2:44

4:11 and 1 Peter 2:4,6, in all of which Christ is spoken of under this name... Impossible is it for this to symbolise the spread of the gospel; for, so far from Christians being put in the place of destroying those that bear earthly rule, they are taught submission to the powers that be as ordained of God and their place is to suffer, if needs be, but not to rebel [Rom. 13:1-7; 1 Pet. 2:13-14; of course, there is a limit (Acts 4:18-20; 5:27-32)].

Thus, it is clear that the Lord Jesus is here referred to as coming again – in the day when he shall take to himself his great power and shall reign – when he shall be revealed 'in flaming fire, taking vengeance on them that know not God, and obey not the gospel of our Lord Jesus Christ' (2 Thess. 1:8).[1]

In broad outline, this is my view.

In sharp contrast, we have John Gill's interpretation, found in his *Commentary*:

[Christ's kingdom] was set up in the days of his flesh on earth, though it came not with observation, or was attended with outward pomp and grandeur, it being spiritual, and not of this world; upon his ascension to heaven it appeared greater; he was made or declared Lord and Christ, and his gospel was spread everywhere: in the times of Constantine it was still more glorious, being further extended, and enjoying great peace, liberty, and prosperity: in the times of popish darkness, a stop was put to the progress of it, and it was reduced into a narrow compass; at the Reformation there was a fresh breaking of it out again, and it got ground in the world: in the spiritual reign it will be restored, and much more increased, through the gospel being preached, and churches set up everywhere; and Christ's kingdom will then be more extensive; it will be from sea to sea and from the river to the ends of the earth; it will be more peaceable and prosperous; there will be none to annoy and do hurt to the subjects of it; it will be no more subject to changes and revolutions, but will be in a firm and stable condition; it will be established upon the top of the mountains, and be more visible and glorious, which

---

[1] Samuel Prideaux Tregelles: *Remarks on the Prophetic Visions in the Book of Daniel*, The Sovereign Grace Advent Testimony, London, Seventh Edition, 1965.

Appendix 1:Daniel 2:44

is here meant by its being 'set up': especially this will be the case in the millennium state,[2] when Christ shall reign before his ancients gloriously and they shall reign with him; and this will never be destroyed, but shall issue in the ultimate glory; for now all enemies will be put under the feet of Christ and his church; the beast and false prophet will be no more; and Satan will be bound during this time, and after that cast into the lake of fire and brimstone, with all the wicked angels and men.

I disagree, in almost every particular, with Gill's view.

---

[2] Although Gill's understanding of the millennium is not altogether easy to unravel, he held to an earthly 1000-year reign of the saints with Christ after his return (see 'Of the Millennium, or Personal Reign of Christ with the Saints on the New Earth a Thousand Years' (John Gill: *A Body of Doctrinal Divinity*, 1767).

Appendix 2: Jonathan Edwards

The purpose of this Appendix is to allow an advocate of the Triumph view of church history to set out his case. I have commented from time to time.

The following comes from Jonathan Edwards' *History of Redemption*. Edwards was speaking of how, down the centuries, Christ has stepped into history to move the church (as Edwards saw it) from one stage of glory to another:

> By each of these comings [that is, interventions] of Christ, God works a glorious deliverance for his church. Each of them is accompanied with a glorious advancement of the state of the church.

I take up Edwards' account with the fall of Jerusalem in AD70, the final end of the old covenant – or, as Edwards, with his Reformed covenant-theology view would have mistakenly described it, the final demise of 'the Jewish dispensation of the one covenant of grace':

> The first [intervention by Christ], which ended in the destruction of Jerusalem, was attended with bringing the church into the glorious state of the gospel, a glorious state of the church very much prophesied of old, whereby the church was advanced into far more glorious circumstances than it was in before under the Jewish dispensation.

As I have made clear in many works, I disagree very strongly with this way of dismissing the radical discontinuity between the old and new covenants.[1] Israel was not 'the Jewish church' (something which never existed), and the old and new covenants, though there is some continuity between them, are radically discontinuous. The new-covenant economy and the gospel is not a more glorious version of the old-covenant

---

[1] See, principally, my *Christ*. But see also my *'A Gospel Church'*.

183

Appendix 2: Jonathan Edwards

economy and the law. To think it is runs utterly contrary to Scripture.

Edwards then moved his account to the fourth century:

> The second [great intervention by Christ], which was in Constantine's time, was accompanied with an advancement of the church into a state of liberty from persecution, and the countenance of civil authority, and triumph over their heathen persecutors.

It is true, of course, that Constantine ended the dreadful persecution of believers under Diocletian, but that certainly did not spell the end of all persecution! Moreover, Constantine's actions led very rapidly to the setting up of Christendom – the major disaster of this present age.

It is at this point that Edwards was showing his prophetic hand, his postmillennialism; namely, he was predicting a glorious period for the church before Christ's return:

> The third [great intervention by Christ], which shall be at the downfall of antichrist, will be accompanied with an advancement of the church into that state of the glorious prevalence of truth, liberty, peace, and joy, that we so often read of in the prophetic parts of Scripture.

After which, Christ will come:

> The last [intervention by Christ] will be attended with the advancement of the church to consummate glory in both soul and body in heaven...

Having set out the general scheme as he saw it, Edwards retraced his steps to make specific points.

First, Constantine:

> There are several things which I would take notice of which attended or immediately followed Constantine's coming to the throne. (1). The Christian church[2] was thereby wholly

---

[2] Edwards was distinguishing between the so-called Jewish church and the Christian church. This takes us back to the previous note, which see.

Appendix 2: Jonathan Edwards

> delivered from persecution. Now the day of her deliverance came after such a dark night of affliction. Weeping had continued for a night, but now deliverance and joy came in the morning. Now God appeared to judge his people, and repented himself for his servants, when he saw their power was gone, and that there was none shut up or left. Christians had no persecutions now to fear.

I must break in. I should like to see Edwards telling this to the countless number tortured, butchered or burnt to death under Roman persecution, the Spanish Inquisition, or to believers today in, say, China, North Korea, parts of Africa, and so on. 'Christians had no persecutions now to fear'? Really! Which part of cloud-cuckoo land was Edwards living in?

Edwards:

> Their persecutors now were all put down, and their rulers were some of them Christians like themselves.

There is some truth in Edwards' claim, I concede as above; with Constantine, some persecution did cease – for a time. But I very seriously question that Constantine was converted.

Edwards moved on to the second and subsequent gains (as he saw them) under Constantine:

> (2). God now appeared to execute terrible judgments on their [that is, believers'] enemies. Remarkable are the accounts which history gives us of the fearful ends to which the heathen emperors, and princes, and generals, and captains, and other great men came, who had exerted themselves in persecuting the Christians, dying miserably, one and another, under exquisite torments of body, and horrors of conscience, with a most visible hand of God upon them. So that what now came to pass might very fitly be compared to their hiding themselves in the dens and rocks of the mountains.

Next:

> (3). Heathenism now was in a great measure abolished throughout the Roman empire. Images were now destroyed, and heathen temples pulled down. Images of gold and silver were melted down, and coined into money. Some of the chief

of their idols, which were curiously wrought, were brought to Constantinople, and there drawn with ropes up and down the streets for the people to behold and laugh at. The heathen priests were dispersed and banished.

Well, that's a highly-selective reading of history!

Edwards went on:

(4). The Christian church[3] was brought into a state of great peace and prosperity. Now all heathen magistrates were put down, and only Christians were advanced to places of authority all over the empire. They had now Christian presidents, Christian governors, Christian judges and officers, instead of their old heathenish ones. Constantine set himself to put honour upon Christian bishops or ministers, and to build and adorn churches. And now large and beautiful Christian churches were erected in all parts of the world, instead of the old heathen temples. This revolution was the greatest revolution and change in the face of things that ever came to pass in the world since the flood. Satan, the prince of darkness, that king and god of the heathen world, was cast out. The roaring lion was conquered by the Lamb of God, in the strongest dominion that ever he had, even the Roman empire. This was a remarkable accomplishment of Jeremiah 10:11: 'The gods that have not made the heavens and the earth, even they shall perish from the earth, and from under these heavens'. The chief part of the world was now brought utterly to cast off their old gods and their old religion, to which they had been accustomed much longer than any of their histories give an account of. They had been accustomed to worship the gods so long, that they knew not any beginning of it. It was formerly spoken of as a thing unknown for a nation to change their gods (Jer. 2:10-11), but now the greater part of the nations of the known world were brought to cast off all their former gods. That multitude of gods that they worshipped were all forsaken. Thousands of them were cast away for the worship of the true God, and Christ the only Saviour. And there was a most remarkable fulfilment of that in Isaiah 2:17-18: 'And the loftiness of man shall be bowed down, and the haughtiness of men shall be made low: and the Lord alone shall be exalted in that day. And the idols he shall utterly

---

[3] See earlier note.

abolish'. And since that, it has come to pass, that those gods that were once so famous in the world, as Jupiter, and Saturn, and Minerva, and Juno, *etc.* are only heard of as things which were of old. They have no temples, no altars, no worshippers, and have not had for many hundred years. Now is come the end of the old heathen world in the principal part of it, the Roman empire. And this great revolution and change of the state of the world, with that terrible destruction of the great men who had been persecutors, is compared, in Revelation 6, to the end of the world, and Christ's coming to judgment, and is what is most immediately signified under the sixth seal, which followed upon the souls under the altar crying: 'How long, O Lord, holy and true, do you not avenge our blood on them that dwell on the earth?' This vision of the sixth seal, by the general consent of divines and expositors, has respect to this downfall of the heathen Roman empire. Though it has a more remote respect to the day of judgment, or this was a type of it. The day of judgment cannot be what is immediately intended, because we have an account of many events which were to come to pass under the seventh seal, and so were to follow after those of the sixth seal. What came to pass now is also represented by the devil's being cast out of heaven to the earth. In his great strength and glory, in that mighty Roman empire, he had as it were exalted his throne up to heaven. But now he fell like lightning from heaven, and was confined to the earth. His kingdom was confined to the meaner and more barbarous nations, or to the lower parts of the world of mankind. This is the event foretold, Revelation 12:9, *etc.* 'And the great dragon was cast out, that old serpent, called the devil and Satan, which deceives the whole world: he was cast out into the earth, and his angels were cast out with him', *etc.* Satan tempted Christ, and promised to give him the glory of the kingdoms of the world. But now he is obliged to give it to him even against his will. This was a glorious fulfilment of that promise which God made to his Son, that we have an account of in Isaiah 53:12: 'Therefore will I divide him a portion with the great, and he shall divide the spoil with the strong; because he has poured out his soul unto death: and he was numbered with the transgressors, and he bare the sin of many, and made intercession for the transgressors'. This was a great fulfilment of the prophecies of the Old Testament concerning the glorious time of the gospel, and particularly of the prophecies of Daniel. Now the kingdom of heaven is come

Appendix 2: Jonathan Edwards

in a glorious degree. It pleased the Lord God of heaven to set up a kingdom on the ruins of Satan's kingdom. And such success is there of the purchase of Christ's redemption, and such honour does the Father put upon Christ for the disgrace he suffered when on earth. And now see to what a height that glorious building is erected, which had been building ever since the fall.

Phew! Edwards clearly saw Constantine as a massive advance for the church, the best thing before sliced bread! As I have argued in many works – and earlier in this present volume – the fact is, Constantine, with his contribution to the invention of Christendom, inflicted a terrible curse on the *ekklēsia*, in particular, and the world, in general. Christendom, with its establishment of the laity/clergy split, hierarchy, the virtual elimination of the priesthood of all believers – replacing it with priestcraft, the absolute dominance of the monologue sermon – sacramentalism, sacerdotalism, vicious persecution of nonconformist believers,[4] the rise of Romanism, infant sprinkling with baptismal regeneration, the erection of sacred buildings, and the like – what a catalogue![5] Each of the disasters in that list would have made enough trouble for the *ekklēsia*; in combination, words fail!

Not for Edwards; he continued:

Inference. From what has been said of the success of the gospel from Christ's ascension to the time of Constantine, we may deduce a strong argument of the truth of the Christian religion, and that the gospel of Jesus Christ is really from God... The gospel's prevailing as it did against such powerful opposition, plainly shows the hand of God. The Roman government, that did so violently set itself to hinder the

---

[4] I do not use the term here in the narrow sense of the 15th-century Separatists and others who refused to conform to the Church of England. I am speaking of those who refuse allegiance to the institutions of Christendom. In the early days, the Donatists; later, the Albigenses and Waldensians, Lollards and Hussites, Anabaptists, and so on.
[5] See, for instance, my *The Pastor*; *The Priesthood*; *Priesthood*; *Infant*; *Battle*; *Laying*; *Luther on Baptism*.

success of the gospel, and to subdue the church of Christ, was the most powerful human government that ever was in the world. And not only so, but they seemed as it were to have the church in their hands. The Christians were mostly their subjects, under their command, and never took up arms to defend themselves; they did not gather together, and stand in their own defence. They armed themselves with nothing but patience, and such like spiritual weapons. And yet this mighty power could not conquer them. But, on the contrary, Christianity conquered them. The Roman empire had subdued the world. They had subdued many mighty and potent kingdoms. They subdued the Grecian monarchy, when they were not their subjects, and made the utmost resistance. And yet they could not conquer the church which was in their hands, but, on the contrary, were subdued, and finally triumphed over by the church.

Not only that:

> No other sufficient cause can possibly be assigned of this propagation of the gospel, but only God's own power. Nothing else can be devised as the reason of it but this. There was certainly some reason. Here was a great and wonderful effect, the most remarkable change that ever was in the face of the world of mankind since the flood. And this effect was not without some cause. Now, what other cause can be devised but only the divine power? It was not the outward strength of the instruments which were employed in it. At first, the gospel was preached only by a few fishermen, who were without power and worldly interest to support them. It was not their craft and policy that produced this wonderful effect. For they were poor illiterate men. It was not the agreeableness of the story they had to tell to the notions and principles of mankind. This was no pleasant fable. A crucified God and Saviour was to the Jews a stumbling block, and to the Greeks foolishness. It was not the agreeableness of their doctrines to the dispositions of men. For nothing is more contrary to the corruptions of men than the pure doctrines of the gospel. This effect therefore can have proceeded from no other cause than the power and agency of God. And if it was the power of God that was exercised to cause the gospel to prevail, then the gospel is his word. For surely God does not use his almighty power to promote a mere imposture and delusion.

Appendix 2: Jonathan Edwards

Edwards saw this as fulfilment of Christ's prophecy:

> This success is agreeable to what Christ and his apostles foretold. Matthew 16:18: 'Upon this rock will I build my church: and the gates of hell shall not prevail against it'. John 12:24: 'Verily, verily I say unto you, Except a corn of wheat fall into the ground, and die, it abides alone: but if it die, it brings forth much fruit'. And John 12:31-32: 'Now is the judgment of this world: now shall the prince of this world be cast out. And I, if I be lifted up from the earth, will draw all men unto me'. John 16:8: 'When he (the Comforter) is come, he will reprove the world of sin, of righteousness, and of judgment – because the prince of this world is judged'. So Paul, in 1 Corinthians 1:21-28 declares, how that after the world by wisdom knew not God, it pleased God, by the foolishness of preaching, to save them that believe, and that God chose the foolish things of the world, to confound the wise, and weak things of the world, to confound the things which are mighty, and base things of the world, and things which are despised, yes and things which are not, to bring to naught things that are. If any man foretells a thing, very likely in itself to come to pass, from causes which can be foreseen, it is no great argument of a revelation from God. But when a thing is foretold which is very unlikely ever to come to pass, is entirely contrary to the common course of things, and yet it does come to pass just agreeable to the prediction, this is a strong argument that the prediction was from God. Thus the consideration of the manner of the propagation and success of the gospel during the time which has been spoken of, affords great evidence that the Scriptures are the word of God.

In light of the weight of Scripture I have quoted in the body of this book, I find Edwards' view utterly incredible – not to say, fantastic.

Appendix 3: Crawford Gribben

I have lightly accommodated the words of Crawford Gribben who was writing about Ireland, since what he said applies far wider than that. He wrote:

> Failure... has marked the entire history of the Christendom-church.[1] By definition, it could not be otherwise. 'Christian Ireland' was never all that it should have been... [the truth is, it never existed – DG]. Failure... has marked the entire history of the church in Christendom.[2] By definition, it could not be otherwise.

The idea of a 'Christian Ireland' – or any 'Christian country' – is a myth invented by Christendom; no such country has ever existed, or ever will. But what Gribben says could not be more relevant to Christendom and the church it has produced.

To let Gribben continue:

> Jesus' teachings made no provision for the elaboration of Christian culture, and gave no warrant for that culture to co-opt the structures of pagan religion or the strategies of earthly power. Measured by the standards of the... [the apostolic letters], the church was in ruins long before it became the religion of the Roman Empire, or crossed beyond its boundaries.[3] This ruin was caused by distortions and even denials of the gospel, was manifest in the development of architectural forms, sacramental theories and structures of governance that elevated clergy over laity, and in the turns to persecution that shored up competing quests for power. The source of this failure may be traced to the possibility [too weak – DG] that culture – rather than Scripture – set so much of the church's agenda... As William Kelly... put it: 'Christendom fell away... into the dream of the church triumphant'...[4] Christians should not be astonished at this long

---

[1] Original 'Christian Ireland'.
[2] Original 'Christian Ireland'.
[3] Original adds 'into Ireland'.
[4] William Kelly: *Hebrews*.

Appendix 3: Crawford Gribben

history of failure, or the horrors to which it has given birth. After all, the letter that Paul wrote to the... Christians in Galatia warned that the gospel would be manipulated as much as it would be denied.

I break in to say that this is too weak, even wrong: Paul rebuked the Galatians not because the gospel would be manipulated but because they we are already – 'so soon' – rejecting the apostolic gospel for a false gospel (Gal. 1:6-9).

Moreover, as he warned the Ephesian elders, the apostle knew that after he had left, false teachers would infest the *ekklēsia*, and even some of the elders themselves would become false teachers (Acts 20:29-31). As Gribben put it:

> Paul predicted that leaders within the church would distort the gospel with horrific consequences for everyone who accepted their teaching. Their distortion of the gospel would be marked by a powerful and hypocritical religious moralism, he warned, in which [professing??? – DG] believers would 'fall from grace' by attempting to earn their salvation. Against these dangers, Paul called for Christians to remember that 'a person is not justified by works of the law but through faith in Jesus Christ', who came to 'deliver us from the present evil age' rather than to dominate it [or accommodate it, or adapt to it – DG].[5]

This is the abiding law for all believers: they are, of course, *in* the world, but they are not *of* the world, and must never be *of* the world (John 15:18-19; 17:11,14-19; Rom. 12:1-2). Evangelicals today, however, are increasingly accommodating themselves, the *ekklēsia* and the gospel to worldly principles and ways in order 'to reach' pagans – 'in it to win it' has become 'of it to win it'.

---

[5] Crawford Gribben: *The Rise and Fall of Christian Ireland*, Oxford University Press, Oxford, 2021, pp209-211.

Appendix 4: John Wesley

John Wesley, in his sermon on 2 Thessalonians 2:7, 'The Mystery Of Iniquity', declared:

> How soon did 'the mystery of iniquity' work... and obscure the glorious prospect! It began to work (not openly indeed, but covertly) in two of the Christians, Ananias and Sapphira. 'They sold their possession', like the rest, and probably for the same motive; but afterwards, giving place to the devil, and reasoning with flesh and blood, they 'kept back part of the price'. See the first Christians that 'made shipwreck of faith and a good conscience'... the first that 'drew back to perdition' instead of continuing to 'believe to the' final 'salvation of the soul!' Mark the first plague which infected the... church; namely, the love of money! And will it not be the grand plague in all generations, whenever God shall revive the same work? O believers in Christ, take warning! Whether you are yet but little children, or young men that are strong in the faith, see the snare; your snare in particular – that which you will be peculiarly exposed to after you have escaped from gross pollutions. 'Love not the world, neither the things of the world! If any man love the world', whatever he was in times past, 'the love of the Father is not' now 'in him!'

Wesley went on the speak of the troubles caused by party spirit (Acts 6), the false teaching of the *pseudadelphoi* who argued for the law (Acts 11 and 15),[1] dissension between Paul and Barnabas over John Mark (Acts 15). In *sum*:

> Such is the authentic account of 'the mystery of iniquity' working even in the apostolic churches! – an account given, not by the Jews or heathens, but by the apostles themselves. To this we may add the account which is given by the Head and Founder of the church; him 'who holds the stars in his right hand', who is 'the faithful and true Witness'. We may easily infer what was the state of the church, in general, from the state of the seven churches in Asia. One of these indeed, the church of Philadelphia, had 'kept his word, and had not

---

[1] Wesley wrongly limited this to 'the ceremonial law'.

denied his name' (Rev. 3:8); the church of Smyrna was likewise in a flourishing state: But all the rest were corrupted, more or less; insomuch that many of them were not a jot better than the present race of Christians; and our Lord then threatened, what he has long since performed, to 'remove the candlestick' from them. Such was the real state of the... church, even during the first century.

Wesley contrasted the scriptural record with the rose-tinted view of many:

How contrary is this scriptural account of the ancient Christians to the ordinary apprehensions of men! We have been apt to imagine that the primitive church was all excellence and perfection.

Wesley continued his account until the time of the outbreak of persecution followed by Constantine:

Persecution never did, never could, give any lasting wound to genuine Christianity. But the greatest [wound] it ever received, the grand blow which was struck at the very root of that humble, gentle, patient love which is the fulfilling of the Christian law, the whole essence of true spirituality,[2] was struck in the fourth century by Constantine the Great, when he called himself a Christian, and poured in a flood of riches, honours, and power upon the Christians; more especially upon the clergy... When the fear of persecution was removed, and wealth and honour attended the Christian profession, the Christians 'did not gradually sink, but rushed headlong into all manner of vices'. Then 'the mystery of iniquity' was no more hid, but stalked abroad in the face of the sun. Then, not the golden but the iron age of the Church commenced... At once, in that unhappy age, broke in all wickedness, and every deadly sin: Truth, modesty, and love fled far away, And force, and thirst of gold, claimed universal sway.

Such was Wesley's assessment of Christendom – one with which I concur. He knew, however – and so do I – that other believers adopt a very different stance:

---

[2] Original 'religion'.

And this is the event which most Christian expositors mention with such triumph! Indeed, which some of them suppose to be typified in the Revelation, by 'the new Jerusalem coming down from heaven!'

Wesley would not budge:

> Rather say it was the coming of Satan and all his legions from the bottomless pit: Seeing from that very time he has set up his throne over the face of the whole earth, and reigned over the Christian as well as the pagan world with hardly any control. Historians, indeed, tell us, very gravely, of nations, in every century, who were by such and such (saints without doubt! [Wesley was being ironical – DG]) converted to Christianity: But still these converts practised all kinds of abominations, exactly as they did before; no way differing, either in their tempers or in their lives, from the nations that were still called heathens. Such has been the deplorable state of the [so-called – DG] Christian Church, from the time of Constantine till the Reformation. A Christian nation, a Christian city... was nowhere to be seen; but every city and country, a few individuals excepted, was plunged in all manner of wickedness.
>
> Has the case been altered since the Reformation? Does 'the mystery of iniquity' no longer work in the Church? No: the Reformation itself has not extended to above one third of the Western Church: so that two thirds of this remain as they were; so do the Eastern, Southern, and Northern Churches. They are as full of heathenish, or worse than heathenish, abominations, as ever they were before. And what is the condition of the Reformed Churches? It is certain that they were reformed in their opinions, as well as their modes of worship. But is not this all? Were either their tempers or lives reformed? Not at all. Indeed many of the Reformers themselves complained, that 'the Reformation was not carried far enough'. But what did they mean? Why, that they did not sufficiently reform the rites and ceremonies of the Church. You fools and blind! to fix your whole attention on the incidentals of religion! Your complaint ought to have been, the essentials of true spirituality[3] were not carried far enough! You ought vehemently to have insisted on an entire change of men's tempers and lives; on their showing they had 'the mind

---

[3] Original 'of religion'.

Appendix John Wesley

that was in Christ', by 'walking as he also walked'. Without this, how exquisitely trifling was the reformation of opinions and rites and ceremonies!

Wesley has made a telling point. It is one thing to change outward behaviour – witness the many twists and turns demanded of the *hoi polloi* in their observance of 'public worship' in England during the 16th century – but a change of heart? How many during the reign of Elizabeth, for political reasons became nominal Protestants but, in heart, in reality, remained Romanists![4] A change of outward behaviour can be coerced; a change of heart is God the Sprit's prerogative.[5]

Wesley:

> Now, let any one survey the state of Christianity in the Reformed parts of Switzerland; in Germany, or France; in Sweden, Denmark, Holland; in Great Britain and Ireland. How little are any of these Reformed Christians better than heathen nations! Have they more, (I will not say, communion with God, although there is no Christianity without it,) but have they more justice, mercy, or truth, than the inhabitants of China or Hindustan? O no! we must acknowledge with sorrow and shame, that we are far beneath them!...
> Is not this the falling away or apostasy from God, foretold by... Paul in his second letter to the Thessalonians? (2 Thess. 2:3.) Indeed, I would not dare to say, with George Fox, that this apostasy was universal; that there never were any real Christians in the world, from the days of the apostles till his time. But we may boldly say that wherever Christianity has spread, the apostasy has spread also; insomuch that, although there are now, and always have been, individuals who were real Christians; yet the whole world never did, nor can at this day, show a Christian country or city.

---

[4] In truth, a great many.
[5] I know of a case where a father demanded that his young son stood during hymn singing, when the boy wanted to sit. He conformed to his father's wishes, but was heard to say that while he was standing outside, he was sitting inside.

Appendix John Wesley

How stupid, then, how wrong, according to Wesley for anybody to talk of 'a Christian England' or 'a Christian America'. For what it is worth, Wesley has my endorsement!

Appendix 5:
B.W.Newton and H.Borlase

We know that:

> ...in... 1834... four [brothers, believers], J.L.Harris, B.W.Newton, H.Borlase, and T.Dowglass, arranged a meeting in Plymouth, to which many Christian ministers were invited, as well as others, and many attended. From notes taken at the meeting, the following answers were prepared by B.W.Newton and H.Borlase.

Having set out the original state of the *ekklēsia*, Newton and Borlase went on:

> The church did not long continue in [its original] state: it needs only [that is, it is only necessary] to compare its present condition with its character and order as [set out in Scripture], to show that now it does not agree with it in one single particular: 'While men slept the enemy sowed the tares'. Many, it may be, will argue *a priori* against the standing fact of the apostasy, which actually took place, as though the promise of Christ: 'Lo, I am with you always', must in this case have failed; but the declension is not only prophesied of in the apostolic letters, but all the seeds of the future evil are clearly disclosed in them. And these, like so many tributary streams, found their way into one mighty current, and gradually bore the church away from the position in which it was originally placed. The history of the three first centuries is an illustration of this. We see in this history how the mischiefs which had begun in the very days of the apostles – divisions, heresies, Judaising, philosophy, and vain deceit; self-exaltation, false teaching, holding the truth in licentiousness, and the absurd wanderings of the human intellect – all rapidly grew up. But worldly glory was the last of all. The church had been corrupted within; the foundation had been undermined: her union in the resurrection of Christ was forgotten; and when the barriers with which God had surrounded her were subverted, the world found an easy entrance. What was the apostasy of the Jews [in the days of the old covenant]? It was this: 'They were mingled among the heathen, and learned their

Appendix 5: B.W.Newton and H.Borlase

works'. The church did the same thing; and this is the essence of its apostasy, the true secret of its fall; for apostasy is departure from the standard laid down by God in principle and practice.

We may remark that as soon as the Spirit ceased to be amongst them, giving real moral power, that men began to claim OFFICIAL authority from the ordination of men. The period of Constantine, perhaps, may be fixed on as the consummation of the church's fall; for... first it became possessed of legalised power, and professedly ceased to be distinctively separate from the world. The apostasy was finally brought into a systematic form in popery...

There are however three features which should be noticed, pre-eminently distinguishable in popery; but which, wherever found, are sure signs of apostasy:

I. The world is identified with the church.

II. The constitution, rites, *etc.* of the... church, which is [that is, that which it was originally – DG] elected and spiritual, is [now – DG] founded on the model of the ancient Jewish system, which was national and outward.

III. Official appointment or ordination is considered to bestow authority, although every spiritual and moral qualification be wanting.

These three evil features are found as decidedly in modern national [Church] systems, as [they are] in the Church of Rome... With respect to the second point, sufficient has been said; only it may be observed that all national [Church] systems have been based upon the *supposed* resemblance between the Christian and Jewish systems, which however are so totally dissimilar, that the principle of the old covenant[1] becomes apostasy in [that is, if it is inserted into] this [that is, the new covenant]. The Jewish system was intended to be of this world. [I think this means either that the old covenant was an external covenant, or it is a reference to the institution devised by the Fathers – that this institution is Jewish]. At the Reformation the principles of individual salvation were recovered; but the Reformation did not take the systems out of the world, but left them where they were before. And this point is of infinite importance. The true view of our present state depends upon it.

---

[1] Originally 'last dispensation'.

Appendix 5: B.W.Newton and H.Borlase

There was then no gathering of God's children together out of the world. The world was still allowed to clothe itself with the garments of the church.

But to come more immediately to our present state.

In what follows, the writers speak of 'National establishments' or 'National churches'. I take this to mean more than The Church of England, for example; I have replaced 'National' with 'Christendom':

> Christendom-establishments are not, like the early churches, united on the ground of belonging to Christ rejected, and risen out of the world because he was disowned by it: but their very principle is to receive the world, and call it by the name of Christ.
>
> Christendom-establishments... do not, like the early churches, 'assemble themselves together', but they assemble with the world...
>
> Christendom-churches receive [those forbidden in Scripture], even at the table of the Lord, to partake of the ONE bread.
>
> They altogether hinder the free course of the Spirit. In the early churches all, whom the Spirit had qualified, were allowed to speak, 'one by one, that all might learn, and all might be comforted' (1 Cor. 14:31). In Christendom-churches none are allowed to speak except one, who professes to have the full authority of the Holy Spirit, though he may have been appointed only by man, and have no spiritual or even moral qualification whatsoever. What would an apostle say to these things? Everything which he had forbidden, would be found to be done; and everything which he had commanded, would be found undone. What is apostasy, except departure in principle and practice from the directions of God?...
>
> The church has forgotten that its only hope is in the resurrection; and as a natural consequence, is looking for rest upon the earth... The church has lost her power and her unity...
>
> The Holy Spirit has not left the church: he has been grieved, but he has not departed; otherwise there would be no church at all. The promise still remains: 'Wheresoever two or three are gathered together in my name there am I in the midst of them', and the blessing of his presence will be known just in proportion as it is looked for and depended on. It is still possible to meet together and follow his commandments to the very letter: and although those gifts may be withdrawn which

Appendix 5: B.W.Newton and H.Borlase

formerly made the church a wonder to the world, yet facts sufficiently show that the gifts of teaching and of speaking to exhortation and comfort, with many others, are still continued in... measure; and it is these which the 'poor of the flock' esteem most precious, as contributing to their growth and instruction in righteousness...
If when the gospel was first preached, a heathen had sought to know what Christianity practically was, he would have found a faithful exhibition of its character in the churches at Antioch or Jerusalem. But the position which was formerly occupied by them is now occupied by the nations of Christendom. From them the heathen have to learn what Christianity practically is... Under the figure of the olive-branch (Rom. 11) and the vine, whose clusters are to be cast into the winepress of wrath, God has recognised the nations as standing in this responsible position. He has also foretold what the end will be; and facts sufficiently show how fearfully the present state of the professing Gentile body agrees with the predicted end... Apostasy can alone account for the present position of the Gentile remnant – united with aliens and separated from one another. Obedience to the word and unanimity in following out its requirements, might yet bring us into a position where we should cease to offend... [and] that it is still possible, even in weakness, to keep 'the unity of the Spirit in the bond of peace', assuming no [human] authority, but looking only to the Holy Spirit to provide what is needed, according as the time requires.[2]

---

[2] B.W.Newton and H.Borlase: *Answers to the Questions considered at a meeting held in Plymouth, on September 15 1834, and the following days; chiefly compiled from notes taken at the meeting*, second edition, Plymouth 1847, emphasis original.

Appendix 6: The English Reformation

In the body of this book, I argued that although the history of Israel in the old covenant, and the history of the *ekklēsia* in the new covenant, both record serious departures from Scripture, even so God used the old-covenant history, and continues to use the unfolding new-covenant history, to bring about his eternal fixed purpose. In this Appendix, I want to argue that the English Reformation serves to illustrate this point: although events were deeply spoiled by sin, even so God brought good from those events, and accomplished his purpose by means of them while he, himself remained untainted. And there is no doubt that although the Reformation was not an unmitigated success, even so God certainly used it – and worked in and through it – to effect massive changes for good. Nowhere is this more true than in England.

I will not repeat the complicated history, but simply try to highlight its significant aspects to make my case. The principal characters in the drama were:

King Henry VIII, an immoral, arrogant, suspicious and dictatorial monarch, who lived and died a Catholic – a Roman Catholic until 1534/5 and, thereafter, an English Catholic with himself as virtual Pope.

Anne Boleyn, daughter of Thomas Boleyn, niece of Thomas Howard – both men playing key roles in the history (see below). She became Henry's second wife in 1533, the pair being openly married by Thomas Cranmer – another key player (see below). She certainly came to adopt evangelical principles, while remaining heavily embroiled in the Catholic religion (she heard mass on the day of her execution, for instance).

Thomas Boleyn, the father of Anne, a power-hungry courtier who made it his ambition to raise his family to high rank within the royal court. In that, he succeeded beyond his wildest

Appendix 6: The English Reformation

dreams, but at awful cost: his daughter Mary became Henry's discarded mistress, his son George was unjustly accused of incest, and beheaded, and his daughter Anne became queen but was executed for alleged adultery, incest and treason.

George Boleyn, son of Thomas, brother of Anne, who rose in influence within the royal court. He came to adopt evangelical views and, by his oratorical skills, played a major role in securing the break of the English Church with Rome, and its submission to Henry as its Supreme Head. He was executed two days before his sister, having been condemned on the false charge of incest with Anne.

Thomas Howard, uncle of Anne, was a ruthless courtier responsible for much of the 'heavy (that is, dirty) work' in Henry's court. It was he who arrested Anne.

Thomas Cromwell, a statesman who rose from lowly birth to become Henry's chief political minister. He was the principal advocate and creator of the English Reformation. It is almost certain that he played a major role in meeting the king's wishes – Henry wanted to be free of Anne and marry Jane Seymour – and thus he engineered Anne's downfall. He himself was executed (after the débacle of his failure over another queen – Anne of Cleves) in 1540.

Thomas Cranmer, a prelate who became the first Archbishop of Canterbury in the English Church. He became resolutely evangelical, and played a major role in doing the king's bidding – which he regarded as his overriding duty – and was, therefore, highly instrumental in bringing about Henry's divorce from his first queen – Catherine of Aragon – which became the catalyst for the English Reformation. Queen Mary, Catherine and Henry's daughter, eventually came to power, and took her revenge, having Cranmer executed in 1556.

William Tyndale, although he was out of the country, nevertheless, with his translation of Scripture from the original languages into English, and with his book *The Obedience of a Christian Man*, had a major influence on Henry through Anne

Appendix 6: The English Reformation

Boleyn, and thus played a major role in the English Reformation.

* * *

The events of Henry's court during the 1520s and 30s were tumultuous for all the characters who played their part in them: many of them having a spectacular rise through the ranks to reach a high – if not the highest – position, but many of them also having catastrophic and precipitate falls, some of them even to the executioner's axe on the block or death by burning at the stake. Leaving aside the characters themselves, England, itself, during those turbulent years underwent the most radical change. While, alas, Christendom maintained its all-dominant hold on State and Church, and although the power of the papacy was not eliminated, nevertheless from the mid 1530s until the present day Rome has never recovered its grip in England, even though it has never ceased trying to regain its power. But the fact is that as a result of those events in Tudor England, millions have come into spiritual liberty and the true experience of Christ and his salvation.

Having said that, my point in this Appendix can be simply stated. All the good that came from the English Reformation – and much good did come from it – *that* good was brought about despite the appalling mix of carnality, political intrigue and manipulation, self-seeking, sexual immorality, cruelty, and the like, during those years when Henry was king. All the parties involved – even the best of them – were utterly blinded by Christendom. I am referring to the misunderstanding and misapplication of Old Testament texts; Cranmer's obsession with carrying out the king's will (his Christendom confusion made him regard such obedience to be God's will); Tyndale's book, which, though so instrumental, was based on Christendom thinking; and so on. In a very real sense, therefore, the events of the English Reformation were an appalling tragedy for all concerned. And yet, even so, without in the least being tainted by sin, God brought immense, long-term good from it.

And that is the point. It illustrates what I said in the body of the book about God bringing good out of both covenants – old and new – despite Israel's apostasy during the time of the former, and the *ekklēsia's* descent into Christendom during the latter.

God is not tainted, nor man exonerated. But God's will is Triumphant.